Pastor First Lady
and
The Church

Dr. Gale Cook Shumaker

DEDICATION

To my parents, the late Emmanuel and the late Annie Mae Crump, the gracious one, thank you for producing such a fruit after your own kind; I hope that you rejoiced because of this seed. Yes, God is indeed with me.

To my husband, Franklin Shumaker, a starter and finisher, gracias! To my seed, Grace Carnetta, who has experienced vicariously a portion of what I've experienced. I pray that you continue to experience God's unmerited favor as you set and reach your goals.

In the power of sisterhood, special thanks to my sisters, the late Jacqueline, late Barbara, Diane, Helen, late Charyle, Yolanda and Lola for their deposits into my life. To my brothers, O'Harold, Larry and Malcolm, you all have been and are indeed, my keeper.

To my spiritual parents, Pastor John O. and Prophetess and Spiritual Godmother, Maybeline Barrentine, thanks for your love, support and prayers.

To my pastor, Apostles Maxine and Johnny Hall and the Full Gospel International Ministry's Church Family, thanks for embracing and supporting me in this endeavors. A special thanks is extended to Prophetess Barbara Moore, Minister E Gray and Elder, Prophetess Iris Crosby for praying that this vision becomes realized.

Contents

Preface

This book addresses interrelationships between pastors, pastors' spouses and church members from both an earthly and a spiritual perspective. The relationships and interrelationships are depictions of corporeality that exist among members in modern day churches. It is a representation of the Gospel that the Lord modeled through the life of Jesus Christ. This book presents both earthly relationships with spiritual implications and spiritual relationships that we as earthly human beings may model within the "get acquainted" period among singles and within the institution of marriage among believers.

Relationships are associations and acquaintances that serve as a bonding revenue for two or more persons. Relationships link actions, the application and the execution of actions or activities. Further, relationships provide a connection, a nexus that produce affiliations and ties. We all coexist and interact with one another through association and relationships.

The lyrics of an old classical song, "No Man is An Island," describe how we as human beings need each other. The lyrics are "no man is an island; No man stands alone.' 'Each man's joy is joy to me; each man's joy is his own." The lyrics emphasize the necessity of human beings' coexistence with others and de-emphasize the indulgence of human beings in a world detached and isolated from others.

In the origin of time as we know it from the scripture, God determined that it was not good for man to be alone. So, God created woman, Eve, a helpmeet for man, Adam. Nonetheless, God provided guidance for the relationship between this man and woman through specific commandments. He commanded the two individuals of this union to: (1) cleave together and become one in marriage; (2) procreate and replenish the earth, and; (3) be fruitful and multiply, in words, deeds and concepts such that the mind conceives, the hand touches and the eye views. This fact further explains that God's intention was for man to coexist with each other. All three aforementioned commandments could be accomplished only by two, a man and a woman, coexistence with one another.

Secondly, prior to creating woman for man, God created all living creatures for man. These creatures include ones that live on land, fly in the air and swim in the water. God also provided guidance for man's relationship with animal. God commanded man to rule over the animal; therefore, He commanded man to have dominion over every living creature that live on land, in the air and in the water. God's intention was for man to utilize these creatures for the productivity of mankind. This fact further explains God's intention for man not to only coexist with man but to also coexist with animal and to rule over these warm and cold-blooded creatures: mammals, reptiles and birds.

God's actions and commandments are sheer indicators that the Creator created His creatures to coexist in unity and harmony. Reflect on Noah's days. God commanded Noah to board the Ark with male and female creatures of the same kind as a mean of provision for mankind, to avoid extinction of these creatures and to escape the great flood (Genesis 7:1-9, 17). God's commandment to Noah depicted the necessity of man, his creation, and animals, his creatures, to exist in unity for the sole purpose of fulfilling the theory of supply and demand.

The Creator commanded His creations to coexist because of needs and demands. Because of this fact, we indeed, "need one another" to fulfill God's initial commandments that were given to the First Adam and Mother Eve. These specific commandments have since been utilized as principles to govern the institution of marriage.

In reference to relationships, interrelationships and interaction in our environment, there are no accidents or coincidences. Those occurrences that one labels incidents or accidents are fate occurring in many different forms such as doom, destiny, lot, foreordination, predestination, predetermination, failure, disaster, crisis, misfortune, fortune, luck, mishap, happenstance, coincidence, chance, providence, precaution, serendipity, grace, miracle, etc. Furthermore, occurrences that are labeled incidents and accidents are not isolated. "Things" just don't happen. Some actions and occurrences are a direct and indirect result of choices. Other occurrences are predetermined. However, actions and occurrences happen with timing and purpose. "To everything there is a season and a time to every purpose under the heaven" (Ecclesiastes 1:1).

Occurrences, labeled as accidents, are sheer messages for one to slow down, speed up, or stay on pace; accidents may send the message that one needs to make a change---to do an opposite action or to redirect or delay activities. Simply, I believe that God is speaking when the unthinkable, the unimaginable and the incredible happen. I believe that "accidents" send a message to the receiver to either smell the petals of the rose, to touch not the thorns of the rose or just to behold the beauty and variety of roses.

In this book, Pastor, First Lady and the Church, I purpose to bridge the gap between what gospels is preached, how to fulfill the gospel that's preached and how to implement the gospel into daily living and practice. Oftentimes, Christians are taught the principles and truths of the Holy Bible but are not taught the ways, methods, lifestyle or the daily practices of fulfilling the principles and truths. The message is proclaimed but the method is not explained.

Further, this book serves as a catharsis and a bibliotherapy during this period of my life. Although, I live a very private life and am a very private person, many personal accounts of my life are featured in this publication for the sake of catharsis—for venting, purification, and finally eviction. Experiencing many unpleasantries, has taught me to divulge the secret episodes which need to be shared for the purposes of: 1) edification, exhortation and comfort to (I Corinthians 14:3) my brothers and sisters in Christ; and, 2) overcoming all hindrances to my personal success and growth both naturally and spiritually. I have learned and am continuously learning more and more each day on how to take the double cross away from the adversary. Those secret episodes that the adversary might use to torment, vex and to control one, are the episodes that I make haste to share with mature individuals. In divulging these episodes or testimonies, one receives an emotional release and a spiritual healing. We overcome the adversary's strongholds by the blood of the Lamb and the words of our testimonies (Revelation 12:11).

Finally, this book is by no means a tool to exonerate me from an error in my life. However, the era in which we live is an era of errors even in the lives of Saints. Simply, life is an era of errors. By God's grace, we may get it right the second time. However, we have the confidence of knowing that through the Holy Spirit we can obtain perfection. Nonetheless, the wealth of knowledge, wisdom and understand acquired during this ordeal has made me spiritually rich, a millionaire, and has added only temporary sorrow. Furthermore, I chose to receive my healing through this form of therapy, writing–venting.

Many pastors, first ladies and church members endure painful situations that they chose not to share for many reasons. Although, we vent our pains to the Lord via our personal relationships and daily fellowship in prayer, "no man is an island and/or stands alone; we all need one another." Therefore, we must find someone whom we trust to become our sounding board for venting pain. One would be astonished to discover that the person with whom the Holy Spirit leads you to share, may need to hear your testimony concerning a shared issue.

Finally, Pastor, First Lady and the Church serves to communicate that one is not alone in a battle. The Lord is a very presence help in times of trouble. Further, the Lord will fight one's battle when the burdens are cast upon him. As cynical as it may sound, many people will be appalled as well as consoled when they discover through this sharing process that similar situations are occurring in their life.

These occurrences are banal, ephemeral, and ubiquitous. Remember, all situations are commonplace, short-lived and wide-spread. Therefore, forget not to cast your burden unto the Lord and experience his sustaining power. God does care for you and your issues.

Pastors, First Ladies and Church members, I encourage each of you to bask in the presence of the Lord to receive a healing and cleansing of your internal wounds. So, crawl up in your Daddy's lap with a hot cup of peppermint herbal tea and receive your healing. Green tea with lemon is also good. Enjoy!

Dr. Gale Cook Shumaker

Introduction

ReGale

Today is my birthday!

I celebrate life!

I celebrate my womanhood!

Life is beautiful and life is free!

For now I know the truth;

Yes, indeed I am free!

I am free as the water that flows in Niagara Falls.

I am free as the world is wide and as the sky is blue!

I am free as the day is light and as the night is black!

I am free as the grass that grows and as time is eternity.

I am as free as the rushing and mighty WIND on the day of Pentecost!

My Great Adonai has set me free!

Whom God has set free is free indeed!

I am GALE and I am free!

The Truth has made me free!

Gale is Free!

_____

My Adonai and Lord:

I pray that I am as King David, the apple of your eye. Further, I pray that I am as an apple, a fruit which may be utilized in many ways. I pray that I continue to produce in my season and become as any form of an apple that's needed to prepare the way for your return and the building of the kingdom. Whether, I become

as an

a p

p l

e

cobbler, apple preserve, or
any type of apple dessert with
added ingredients; or as an apple
fruit or salad, served baked, raw, natural,
processed, dried, spiced, canned, sauced;
or as an apple jolly rancher, caramel apple,
red candied apple, or any kind of apple
that's prepared as hardened apple candy,
or even perhaps apple cider; or apple
juice or any form of apple drink; or the
symbolism of a teacher's apple; or
the daily apple that keeps the
d o c t o r   a w a y,
my prayer is for God to
continue to season me for service. I'm available!

PART ONE

1 Season, Time and Purpose

A time to love, and a time to hate; a time of war and a time of peace; (Ecclesiastes 3:8).

King Solomon declares in the book of Ecclesiastes that there are no accidents or incidents. Occurrences, labeled accidents and incidents are the manifestation of fate in its own decree. These accidents and incidents, commonly known as an "it, that, thing, doom, destiny, lot, foreordination, predestination, predetermination, happenstance, coincidence, chance, providence, reaping, serendipity, grace and miracle" usually manifest themselves in the form of blessing, success, feat, fortune, luck, woe, failure, loss, hardship, disaster, crisis, mishap, persecutions, trials and tribulations. King Solomon called these accidents and occurrences "things" or "everything."

Accidents and incidents are not isolated. "Things" just don't happen. Occurrences are well orchestrated in time and space by the Master of Father Time. Occurrences happen during an appointed seasons, at a fixed time and with a general or specific purpose. Some occurrences are a direct or an indirect result of choices or the failure to choose; others are predetermined. However, occurrences happen with precise timing and with a definite purpose. "To everything there is a season and a time to every purpose under the heaven" (Ecclesiastes 3:1). Furthermore, chance happens to us all. What we call accidents and incidents are sheer messages for one to slow down the pace for self-examination, speed up the pace for fulfilment of one's destiny, or to simply stay on pace of the divine ordination. Perhaps, accidents relay the message that a change is needed: an opposite, redirected or delayed action is needed.

Accidents communicate the message to the receiver to smell the petals of the rose, to touch not the thorns of the rose or just to admire the beauty and variety of roses. Simply, I believe that God is speaking when the unthinkable, the unimaginable and the incredible happen.   When an explanation isn't to be found for an occurrence, why seek one.   Just trust, my Adonai, who is the great Orchestrator. Accept this occurrence as being a preordination.

2 My Adonai

So it happened to me. Why not me? God has endowed me with the spiritual consciousness, intuition and spiritual weapons to handle any, rather all situations that come to test and try my faith. From the world order system's perspective and mine, I must value at a high price; for, I have been tried in the fire all my life. "The trial of my faith, being much more precious than of gold that perisheth, though it is tried with fire, might be found as praise and honor and glory at the appearance of Jesus Christ" (I Peter 1:7).

God has polished and refined me, since my spiritual calling, as a piece of pure gold who is ready and willing to do God's business (Saint Luke 2:49), will and work (Saint John 4:34). Because of ongoing persecutions, trials, and tribulations for righteousness' sake, for the glory of God and for God's love for the world, I've inherited the spiritual right and the born-again privilege to become a child of the King and a child of His kingdom. I am an affirmed Believer that Christians who specified purpose is to up hold the blood stain banner of Christ, to live during this appointed season as the scripture prescribed, and to witness at this fixed time about the gospel of Christ, suffer mightily at the hand of the adversary. This suffering comes simply because of their divine purpose, spiritual agenda and calling and ordained mission."For the kingdom of heaven suffered violence and the violent took it by force since the days of John the Baptist" (Saint Matthew 11:12). Persons who are genuinely children of God and whose agenda is to prepare for the King and His kingdom have endured violent assaults without a malicious cause or any cause; furthermore, all God's children who are for the occasion and endeavor to build the kingdom which is to come will suffer or have suffered vindictive violence repetitively as the cankerworm, the locust and the palmerworm constantly took from them (Joel 2).

The second Epistle of Paul to the Thessalonians supports the claim of suffering for righteousness' sake. Paul said:

> 1:4 "So that we ourselves glory in you in the churches of God for your patience and faith in all your persecutions and tribulations that ye endure (suffer);

> 1:5 which is a manifested token of the righteous judgment of God, that ye may be counted worthy of the kingdom of God, for which ye also suffer (forbear);

> 1:6 Seeing it is a righteous thing with God to recompense (repay) tribulations to them that trouble

you;" (Nelson, 1981).

God rewards His children and replaces double-fold anything that the cankerworms take.

In the Book of Job, Job, a perfect and upright servant of God who eschewed evil, is a great depiction of how the canker and palmer worms took Job's acquired possessions at the permission of God. Also, the story of Job highlights how humans prejudge one another during mishaps. King Solomon supports Job's suffering for righteousness in the following scripture. Solomon stated that,

> 7:15 "All things have I seen in the days of my vanity: there is a just man that perisheth in his righteousness, and there is a wicked man that prolongeth his life in his wickedness" (Ecclesiastes).

However, God replaced to Job, double the amount of his loss. Furthermore, God multiplied all of Job's possessions that were taken by satan. Job received the same amount of children, twice as many cattle, restored health and wealth. The Book of Job is a good illustration of how satan can only come against God's children after permission is granted by God. Read the Book of Job to acquire greater insight of God's restoration of all that satan killed, stole and destroyed.

I have fought constant combat against principalities,

powers and rulers in high places in order to receive and enjoy my spiritual inheritance and just earthly rewards. God's children are in constant warfare just to live peaceably with men. I fought spiritual warfare minute-by-minute and day-by-day as I repeatedly enjoyed the "good of the land" and the benefits of sowing. My warfare is ongoing in this area and accomplished in a few; Jesus fought my battle and I am victorious. God allowed me the victory; therefore, He too, was victorious and glorified.

> *"I know the devil and the devil knows me!*
>
> *I breathe God; for it was God who blew life back into me.*
>
> *I feast on God, as I meditate on His Word day and night.*
>
> *I live for God, dwelling in the house of God:*
>
> *Inquiring about His secrets and mysteries that are made*
>
> *known only to a few, His called, chosen, and elected ones."*

My Adonai, my Master and Lord, knew He could trust me to do the right things concerning my life; that is, make the right choices that would render Jesus the glory. God didn't allow satan to put any more on me than my fragile and feeble self could handle. In some of my life's situations, Jesus made a narrow way for me to escape. Yes, my Adonai gave me not just one way, but many ways to escape and survive the enemy's snares.

The escapes from the devil's snares were great; for satan, his imps and demons worked to imprison my soul and spirit both day and night as he does all of God's saints. I surrendered completely to My Adonai as He loosed and set me free. The regeneration process concluded with my freedom in the Holy Spirit and with my development into a spiritual woeman. I now realize that to live in bondage is a choice as it is to live in liberality.

The war and battles were unfamiliar to me but not my Master, my Adonai. Yes, the war and battles were launched against me, as they are launched against all God's soldiers. My Adonai fought my battles while the Lord, my Shepherd, restored my soul.

> 1:1 "O comfort ye, comfort ye my people says God.
>
> 1:2 Speak comfortably to Jerusalem, and cry unto her, that her warfare is accomplished, that her iniquity is pardoned: for she hath received of the Lord's hand double for all her sins" (Isaiah 40).

As the Lord comforts His people, Jerusalem, and declared warfare is accomplished in their battles, so did God comforted me and accomplished through warfare some things that He promised. Not only did He achieved the aforementioned in my life, the Lord gave to me doubled some of the things that the locust, cankerworm and palmerworm had taken.

PART TWO

3 Man, Like a Tree, Planted

. . . that they might be called trees of righteousness, the planting of the Lord, that he might be glorified (Isaiah 61:3)

I prayed for God to bless me with a mate who is like a tree, well rooted and firmly planted by the rivers of waters (Psalms 1:3). I desired a husband who is grounded in the knowledge and wisdom from God and who is steadfast and unmovable in circumstances. I prayed for a blessed husband who delighted himself in the laws of the Lord and who walked in the counsel of the godly. Subsequently, I prayed for a husband who as a tree, produces ripen fruit in his season and who is known by the fruits he bears (Jeremiah 17:8). I desired a mate who prospers in his ways because he abides in God's will. Moreover, I desired a mate who labors in the vineyard, abounds in the works of the Lord and is covered by the blood of the Lamb.

No, I didn't want a husband who as a seed, must die then grow into a tree. I wanted a seed who had already been planted, germinated, cultivated and had matured into a tree. I wanted a husband who was a product of the seed of David. I desired a tree, a husband who had died to sin and who had matured in Christ Jesus. Inasmuch as God gives the desires of one's heart (Psalms 37:4) and supplies one's needs according to His richest in Glory (Philippians 4:19), I desired a fully developed and ripen tree, husband, who produces the fruit of the Spirit. I wanted the Lord to bless me with a husband who is like a tree, planted by the rivers of waters and who cannot be moved by the cares of this world (Psalms 1).

Heretofore, as the scripture described, I desired a tree, a husband, who has deeply embedded roots in the soil of Christianity. I desired a tree that had grown roots that spread in the vineyard and shared its fruit with the plenteous harvest.

17:8 For he shall be as a tree planted by the waters, and that spreadeth out her roots by the river, and shall not see when heat cometh, but her leaf shall be green; and shall not be careful in the year of drought, neither shall cease from yielding fruit (Jeremiah, KJV).

4 Men as Trees

Many scriptures in the bible view "men as trees" or "men like trees" (Saint Marks 8:24 and Jeremiah 17:8). Old and New Testament scriptures alike use the analogy of "men as trees" or compared unto a tree (Psalms 1:3; 37:35; Ezekiel 17:5-6; 31:3; Jeremiah 22:15; and, Matthew 7:17-19). Old Testament passages describe men as trees, trees as kings, trees as nations of people (Ezekiel 17:24), and trees as kingdoms (Daniel 4).

The Prophet Ezekiel in 17:22-24, compared the eternal kingdom of the Messiah unto a great cedar tree. In Ezekiel 17: 22b-23, the Lord God spoke and stated,

> 22b "thus saith the Lord God, I will also take of the highest branch of the highest cedar, and will set it up; I will crop off from the top of his young twigs a tender one, and will plant it upon an high mountain and eminent;"

> 23 "In the mountain of the height of Israel will I plant it; and it shall bring forth boughs and bear fruit, and be a goodly cedar: and under it shall dwell all fowl of every wind; in the shadow of the branches thereof shall they dwell."

The highest branch in this passage of scripture, is symbolic of the restoration of the Kingdom of Israel and the Tender One is referred to as Jesus Christ. This Tender One, Branch, will become a great cedar tree and bear fruit. Further, the coming Messiah's Kingdom will be established and the Kingdom of David will be rebuilt and Restored (Daniel 4:10-15; 20-26).

Ezekiel 17:24, indicates that nations of people were compared to trees and were symbolic of the kingdoms of the world. It reads, "and all the trees of the field shall know that 'I the Lord have brought down the high tree (Saint Luke 1:52), have exalted the low tree, have dried up the green tree, and have made the dry tree to flourish: I the Lord have spoken and have done it" (KJV).

According to Luke 1:52, the mighty who set on the seat was cast down. The high trees that were abased are symbolic of the Kingdom of Nebuchadnezzar (Daniel 4:24-37), Pharaoh (Exodus 15:1-11), Belshazzar (Daniel 5) and Uzziah (2 Chronicles 26:16). The low tree that was exalted is symbolic of the Messiah's Kingdom and the restoration of the David's Kingdom (Ezekiel 17:22-23). The dried up green tree is symbolic of the Kingdom of Babylon and the dry tree that flourished is symbolic of the Kingdom of the Messiah (Drakes, 1992)

5 Vision of Tree

In the book of Daniel, King Nebuchadnezzar had a vision of a very tall tree. The tree in the dream was representative of a king and his kingdom (Daniel 4:4-26). However, this vision occurred shortly after, King Nebuchadnezzar threw the three Hebrew boys, Shadrach, Meshach and Abednego, into the burning fiery furnace. The three Hebrew boys disobeyed the decree which was to serve King Nebuchadnezzar's gods and to worship the golden image (Daniel 3).

While King Nebuchadnezzar was resting very peacefully in his luxurious palace, he had a very frightful dream of a very tall tree. The dream frightened King Nebuchadnezzar to the degree that he made a decree that summons all the wise men of Babylon to the palace so that they could interpret the dream. Among the wise men were magicians, astrologers, Chaldeans and soothsayers. However, the only person who could interpret the King's dream was Daniel, whose name was Belteshazzar.

So Daniel interpreted King Nebuchadnezzar's dream. The tree, in the dream, had grown so very tall that it reached heaven and could be seen at the ends of the earth. The meaning of the dream was symbolic of King Nebuchadnezzar and his kingdom. King Nebuchadnezzar and his kingdom, like the tree, had grown tall and powerful until it touched heaven and could, therefore, be seen at the different ends of the world. As the dream progressed, the very powerful tall tree was hewn down to a stump. This was symbolic of King Nebuchadnezzar when he was debased after losing his mind. However, the dream and its reality concluded with King Nebuchadnezzar worshiping the True God, the God of the three Hebrew boys, Shadrach, Meshach and Abednego. Read the fourth chapter of Daniel for the details of the story.

6 Men as Walking Trees

Another very familiar New Testament story illustrates the comparison of "men as trees." In Saint Mark 8:22-24, at the Pool of Bethsaida, Jesus performed a miracle on a blinded man. Jesus took the blinded man by the hand and led him outside of town. Then, Jesus spat on the blinded man's eyes and placed his hands upon him. Jesus asked the blinded man "did he see as ought." The blinded man stated, "I see 'men as trees, walking." Jesus place his hands on the blinded man's eyes again. Jesus made the blinded man look up; the blinded man's sight was restored as he saw every man clearly (Saint Mark 8:22-24).

Think for a moment. Did the blinded man see with a spiritual eye the first time Jesus spat on his eyes? Did this blinded man espies as Jesus espies when he saw men as trees? Did Jesus intentionally and partially completed the miracle the first time and had to touch the blinded man's eyes a second time? Or what was the objective of Jesus touching the blinded man's eyes twice? Was a divine and complete healing contingent on the blinded man's unwavering faith? Or was the blinded man faith unwavering? Was this healing based on the "measure of faith" issued to the group of people who brought the blinded man to Jesus? Did Jesus heal the blinded man gradually?

Or, did the blinded man see with natural eyes, as the world views men? Did the blinded man see the first time as God intended him to see? Selah.

Let's closely examine this passage of scripture. A group of people delivered the blinded man unto Jesus at the Pool of Bethsaida and entreated Jesus to touch him. This group of people sought Jesus with such great expectation and faith level that they anticipated a miraculous healing performed by Jesus on the blinded man. They not only asked Jesus to touch the blinded man, they entreated, literally begged or beseeched Jesus to touch him. Jesus isolated the blinded man from the group of people by leading him by the hand outside of town for restoration of sight.

Jesus, first, spat on, and then touched the blinded man's eyes. Jesus, then asked the blinded man did he see as ought. Next, Jesus, touched the blinded man's eyes again and made him look up. The blinded man's sight was restored and he saw every man clearly.

Now think! How did the blinded man know how or what he "ought" to see? Did he know how a tree was supposed to look? Did he know that a man should or should not look like a tree? Did the blinded man know how men were supposed to look? Did the blinded man know that men were supposed to walk and trees were supposed to remain stationary? Yet, the blinded man looked up and said, I see "men as trees", walking. What was the significance of the blinded man seeing or saying he saw "men as trees, walking?" Was this blinded man's statement literately or figuratively? Did the blinded man spiritually discern? What was going on concerning this healing? Selah!

It is discernible that the blinded man had physical eyesight at one time in his life. For how did the blinded man know how men "ought" to look if he never viewed a man with his physical eyesight? Now, he knew how he "felt' he looked" using his sensory perception. But, how could the blinded man compare and contrast the attributes of men with that of trees or the attributes of trees with that of men? Nonetheless, the blinded man stated that he "saw men as trees, walking." Selah.

When Jesus touched the blinded man's eyes the second time, the blinded man not only received his sight, his sight was restored. A restored "sight" indicates that the blinded man once saw or had some dimension of vision and was receiving vision again. Furthermore, after the second laying on of hands, the blinded man saw every man clearly. This indicates that the blinded man saw men plainly and unquestionably as we see men today, and as he once saw men.

It is also discernible that the blinded man had spiritual eyesight. For he knew many things by the unction of the Holy Spirit. The blinded man who could not see, knew that there was a distinct difference in the way men and trees looked. He saw men as trees, tall, stationary, with limbs, branches and fruit; however, the blinded man who could feel the way he looked himself, and knew his attributes, was cognizant that trees did not walk or talk and that man did not resemble a tree. Could this possible mean that when the blinded man saw men clearly that he viewed men the way humans view men? Or could the blinded man possibly, at the point of the laying on of hands, reflected on these two scriptures: Psalms 1:3, and; Jeremiah 17:8.

> 1:3 and he shall be like a tree planted by the rivers of waters, that bringeth forth his fruit in his season; his leaf also shall not wither; and whatsoever he doeth shall prosper (Psalms, KJV)

> 17:8 For he shall be as a tree planted by the waters, and that spreadeth out her roots by the river, and shall not see when heat cometh, but her leaf shall be green; and shall not be careful in the year of drought, neither shall cease from yielding fruit (Jeremiah, KJV).

Perhaps, the blinded man saw men as Jesus viewed men after the first touch? Selah.

7 Men as Trees of Righteousness

In society today and as it was yesterday, men and their seeds or ancestors comprise a family tree. Many cultures trace their family tree through many generations and sometimes are blessed to trace the family tree to its very origin. In some parts of the country and with some cultures, a tree is planted each time a child is born or when there is an addition to the family, either by marriage, birth and or adoption. So men have been and still are referred to or liken unto a tree.

In Psalms 1:1-3 and Jeremiah 17:7-8, "men as trees" and "men like trees" implied that men had an intimate and righteous relationship with God. Men referenced in these passages of scriptures are godly men who trust and hope in the Lord (Jeremiah 17:7). These blessed men delight and meditate in the law of the Lord day and night (Psalms 1:2).

In Isaiah 61:1-3, God anointed men to preach to and win lost souls so that those lost souls also may be called "trees of righteousness." God desired his anointed ones to preach good tidings unto the meek, the brokenhearted and to the captives (Isaiah 61:1). He further desired that the anointed preacher who has "a burden for the lost souls and for the world's conditions" (Dakes, 1992), to comfort those persons who mourned by giving to them beautiful ornament instead of ashes and garments of praise for the spirit of heaviness; God wanted the brokenhearted people to also have the privilege to be called "trees of righteousness," (Isaiah 61:3). This ministry will be established as "the planting of the Lord that he might be glorified (Isaiah 61:3)."

As you can plainly see, many scriptures in the bible view "men as trees" or "men like trees" (Saint Marks 8:24 and Jeremiah 17:8). The Old and New Testament alike use the analogy of "men as trees" or compared unto a tree (Psalms 1:3; 37:35; Ezekiel 17:5-6; 31:3; Jeremiah 22:15; and, Matthew 7:17-19). Further, as was plainly sketched in this section, the bible also described "men as trees", "trees as nations of people" (Ezekiel 17:24), and trees as kingdoms (Daniel 4).

PART THREE

8 My Mate, My Tree

. . . "whosoever finds a wife finds a good thing and obtain favor of the Lord" (Proverb 18:22).

When my mate, my tree entered my life, he appeared to be the answer to my prayers. Initially, his character was aligned with scriptures concerning a good man (Proverbs 12:2a and 6:20) and my character aligned with the scriptures concerning a virtuous woman (Proverb 31). However, there were displayed traits and characteristics that cast doubts on my confidence. I reflected that during my life time, I had not asked the Lord for anything that He didn't give me. Because the Lord answered all my prayers, I reasoned that my mate was my lifelong husband whom God had preordained from the foundation of the world.

At this juncture in my life, I examined the status of the present relationship with my soon-to-be husband. I then realized that I was in too deep to bail out of this relationship. Rather, the adversary caused me to think and feel that I was in too deep. I felt that I was at a point of no return from the mistake that I sensed was about to happen if the marriage took place. Further, I was in a state of anxiety, where doubt had gripped my heart and uncertainty had shaken my confidence. I transformed in a matter of weeks and months from a confident, wholesome, sober and virtuous woman to a doubtful, unstable, unready and intoxicated soon-to-be-bride. I changed from being strong in mental and moral qualities to being weak in judgment and purpose. In essence, I was in dire need for my Savior to rescue me from this horrible pit that I dug. Mistake, Mistake!

However, I know this situation spiritually matured me and increased my faith in many ways. It afforded me the opportunity to completely trust in God and to draw upon His unfailing strength. Further, I must hasten to say as Dr. Peck said in The Road Less Traveled and Beyond, "problems are the cutting edge that distinguishes between success and failure.' 'Problems call forth our courage and wisdom.' 'It is only because of problems that we grow mentally and spiritually" (1977, p. 144). James, a servant of God, sums up the essence of experiences in the following scriptures.

> 1:2 "Count it all joy when you fall into divers' temptations;
>
> 1:3 Knowing this, that the trying of your faith worketh patience.
>
> 1:4 But let patience have her perfect work, that ye may be perfect and entire, wanting nothing (KJV, James 1:2-4)."

Singles, regardless to how closed you are toward the mark of marriage, you are not committed in holy matrimony to the next person until the minister performing the ceremony announces that the two of you are "man and wife." Listen, there is always time to reconsider taking this holy, lifelong vow, prior to saying, "I do." Frankly, you are never too close to reconsider this sacred lifestyle. Remember, the marriage vow involves a lifetime commitment.

9 Proverbs 31 Woman

During the stage of waiting for the right man to discover you, his treasure box and "good thing," both men and women must exercise caution. Firstly, the scripture reads, "whosoever finds a wife finds a good thing and obtain favor of the Lord" (Proverb 18:22). Women, men are on a treasure hunt for a "Proverb 31 woman." Men, you must seek and find a virtuous woman and a good thing. Christian men are looking for the virtuous woman whose price is far above rubies (Proverbs 31). King Lemuel, asked, as he uttered the prophecy that his mother taught him (Proverb 31:1), "who can find a virtuous woman (Proverb 31:10)?" I echo this question, "who will find a virtuous woman?" Men, are you willing to search for a "virtuous woman?"

"Virtuous," in the Hebrew language, "chayil," means strong in all mental and moral qualities. The virtuous woman described in Proverbs 31:10-31, has many mental and moral qualities. Men, women, a virtuous woman, is a wholesome person who executes many mental and moral duties on a daily basis. The virtuous woman is described by King Lemuel as a good help-meet, mother, worker, merchant, trader, gardener, marketer, seamstress and craftswoman. Further the virtuous woman is a businesswoman, real estate dealer, marketer, supervisor and distributor. She is wise, loyal, regal, royal, yet holy. She is blessed and highly favored woman of God. "Men, will you have patience until you find a virtuous woman? Women, can you maintain your virtue until you are found? Again I ask, who 'can' find a virtuous woman?" Selah!

10 A Virtuous Woman

Ruth, Boaz's wife and Obed's mother, both from the lineage of Jesus (Saint Matthew 1:5), was a virtuous woman. Ruth was a loyal and faithful woman in the bible who is called a "virtuous woman" (Ruth 3:11). Ruth was a young widower who was married until death departed the two; yet, she was called a virtuous woman. Often, the two words, virtuous and virgin, are incorrectly used interchangeably. However, a virgin is not always a virtuous woman and a virtuous woman is not always a virgin.

In Bethlehem, Ruth was known as a virtuous woman because she remained a widow and took care of Naomi, her mother-in-law many years after the death of her husband. Ruth was eventually found gleaning in Boaz's field. The answer to King Lemuel's question, "who can find a virtuous woman?" Boaz found his virtuous woman and good thing.

11 Seek and Find Your Good Thing

Gentlemen, as you search and pray to find the preordained helpmeet, be cognizant of the advice and guidance that the scripture has to offer. In many passages of scripture, the making and stages of many relationship and marriage are told. The stories of Abraham and Sarah, Mary and Joseph, King David and Abigail, Boaz and Ruth, and many others are success stories that shed light to the paths of those who are seeking to find and found their good thing.

The Apostle Matthew who was also called Levi, stated, "seek, and you shall find" (Saint Matthew 7:8). Apostle Matthew further stated that, "he that seeketh findeth and he that asketh, it shall be given unto him" (Saint Matthew 7:9). Be encouraged men! Apostle Matthew is advocating that if one seeks with unwavering faith and great expectations as indicated in this passage, then one will reap the benefit of seeking which is, finding what you seek. In this case scenario, what one seeks and finds is a wife, a good thing; what one shall ask for and receive is a virtuous woman.

King Solomon, known as the wise man who lived and as the king who had 1,000 women, seven hundred wives, princesses and three hundred concubines (I Kings 11:3) offered advice to men concerning women. Solomon, the king whose heart was turned away from God because of the love and influence of strange women stated,

> 7:25 "I applied mine heart to know, and to search, and to seek out wisdom, and the reason of things, and to know the wickedness of folly, even of foolishness and madness:'

> 7:26 'And I find more bitter than death the woman, whose heart is snares and nets, and her hands as bands: whoso pleaseth God shall escape from her; but the sinner shall be taken by her" (Ecclesiastes).

In summation, King Solomon advice is to please God, find a wife, find a good thing and obtain God's favor. For this order is God's perfect will. However, King Solomon cautions men about women whose hearts are snares and nets. He compares a relationship with a woman of that caliber as being bitter as death. He further states that if a man displeases God, he will find and be taken in by this type woman and thereby live a life that is comparable to a bitter death.

12 Hidden Treasure

While women and men are waiting in this hiding-and-seeking and waiting-and-finding stage, we must constantly meditate and pray. Henceforth, women must reason that they are not hidden and therefore cannot be found from a hidden state when they're in the limelight, advertising on their lapels, "single and available." I once met a very special single pastor who stated to me, "You are a hidden box of treasure." What this gentleman implied, in my opinion, is that he was seeking and he did find a "good thing" as he indicated by his description, "a box of treasure."

In a box of treasure, there are many goodies and surprises. Some of the goodies in the treasure box are valued higher than others. There may be also, desirable and undesirable surprises found among the contents of the treasure. Usually the good surprises as well as the entire content of the treasure box (the inner beauty of the woman), are welcomed and are well worth the hunt because your best efforts, time, and prayer should be exerted toward finding this hidden treasure. Even the actual treasure box (the outer beauty of the woman), is viewed as a trophy or in this case a good thing. Furthermore, the seeker or man who obtains favor and perseveres or endures to the end shall finds the box of treasure which is a wife adorned with Proverb 31 qualities and whose value is far above the price of rubies, my birthstone.

PART FOUR

13 Preparation and Waiting
. . . that you may be perfect and entire, wanting nothing" (James 1:4)

During preparatory, women anxiously wait to be discovered by the husbandman who has obtained favor. However, we must not faint during the process. We must realize that preparation and waiting are stages that must be embraced and utilized to prepare for a lifetime commitment to a person who has a completely different upbringing and set of values and morals.

When we fail to utilize the preparatory period for discovery and exploration of one's self and the study of the scripture, we become desperate for our Boaz or King David and compromise our standards. From the state of desperation, we may settle for a man who is not the ordained groom and one who has not obtained favor of the Lord (Proverb 12:2a). Later, we will live to regret settling with a man who has not obtained that ordained favor.

Secondly, women initially, apply every scripture that's in their repertoire on "how to identify a saved and good man" when they met a gentleman. However, when this man and woman become acquainted through a courtship, all scriptures that are stored in their schemata concerning a godly man are forgotten. Discernment fails to operate, desperation fills the heart and mind and lust enters the eye and body. This waiting period often, climaxes in a compromising predicament. As a result, we settle for what appears to be the ordained husband from God. We may even settle for the seed and not the tree. That is, we may settle for a mate who is somewhat suitable and not the "greater one" whom God has prepared and chosen for us. I remember so very vividly when I sought the Lord concerning marriage, the Holy Spirit gently whispered, "a greater one shall come." I was confident that a "greater one" was prepared for me to marry.

Singles, do not compromise your standards. When doubt enters the decision-making process in marriage, wait for clarity on the matter from the Lord. Apply all scriptures concerning your mate. Marriage is not a temporal setup. Always remember that this decision must become the final decision: a lifelong endeavor. There's no testing the water to see if it works. It is amazing how we are faithful in many areas of the scripture; however, in the area of abstinence, we fail miserably. I say wait on the Lord to send your King David. You'll be much happier if you waited. Selah.

Thirdly, singles have statistically become so vulnerable to the "old maid, use it or lose it syndrome." This assumed weakness causes singles to desire to marry at and for any cause. Singles have become so unrelenting in the decision to marry until insight from the Holy Spirit is ignored. This is an utterly mistake. Although, God may permit a marriage, one should pray that their marriage is in the perfect season and is the perfect will of God. Abraham's Sarah was 90 and had not lost the ability to conceive, bear and rear a child. Therefore, if you think that you better hurry and marry before childbearing days or over, you have time. God still works miracles!

In the process of mate selection, God doesn't fail His children and we should not fail ourselves. God intervenes on the behalf of His children by allowing red flags to surface in courtships that He does not sanction. Furthermore, God warns his children in many ways that we are headed for danger. Red flags serve to inform and to reveal the true character of the mate or of one's prospect. However, because of desperation and anticipation, we make excuses for God's revelations and therefore ignore the red flags concerning the mate and prospect. Many issues may be overlooked concerning a mate who does not aligned with the scripture. Later, we revisit the signs from the Lord with 20-20 hindsight and declare, "I saw it coming."

Fourthly, I have also noticed this trend among women in waiting. Women who are desperately waiting or seeking for Mr. Right will usually accept the first man who comes along who may or may not be the preordained husband. Furthermore, statistically, only a few men are turned down when they ask a woman hand in marriage. On the other hand, men are usually a bit more patience in this process. It may be due to the fact that there is a smaller ratio of men to woman. However, the humbling part of the proposal is, men usually propose to a woman on their knees. Now women propose to men via internet. In this instant "the devil is a liar and the father of all lies" or is it a microwave syndrome?

Just a word of caution woman! Be aware that several men will enter one's life for a specific season and with a definite purpose. Every man who enters a woman's life is not a potential mate and is not the "chosen one." Only one is the preordained chosen mate and has entered for a lifetime. Choose wisely and pray, not faint!

Some men enter a woman's life to witness about the goodness of the Lord. Others are sent to witness about God's loving kindness and tender mercies. Still there are others who enter a woman's life to provide agape love and brotherly companion. Be aware that some men enter a woman life as a wolf wearing sheep clothing. Be assured that a man or woman of this caliber or character does not enter and reside permanently in a Christian's life. Realize the purpose God has for that person in your life as you fulfill God's purpose for your life. Both, the purpose of your life and the purpose a mate has in your life should complement each other. Remember, when a courtship or companionship concludes in marriage, the chosen and ordained person will be there until the end. However, if the selection of the mate is not ordained, the wrong person is usually present in one's life only for a season.

14 Patience's Perfect Work

Be cognizant that the Lord God is omniscience. He knows the status of your life. The Lord and the adversary are both aware when we are lonely, desperate and impatience. Look to the Lord in a time of need. Know that when we are impatience, we make irrational decisions that later cause a lifetime of grief.

Singles wait patiently on the Lord. Purpose to wait during this period of your life. Acquire a waiting and patient spirit. Allow internal changes to occur so that you may enjoy this waiting period. Don't be so quickly to give up your freedom of a single life. Further, allow yourself space for the gift of discernment to operate concerning this important and lifelong commitment. Be aware that all men and women who visit the church in quest for a mate do not love the Lord. Women and men must be aware that some prospects who are coming to the church to find a good, virtuous and saved Christian to marry are not saved themselves. They come to the church to find and subdue God's very best. Be wise as a serpent and harmless as a dove during this period.

Singles again I say, be patient. Let patience have her perfect work in your life. Allow patience to cultivate a complete, holy and an absolute work within you. Submit to patience's perfect work so that you may develop into a, pure, sacred, and an impeccable bride. Fulfill James 1:4 in your life. "Let patience have her perfect work in your life that you may be perfect and entire, wanting nothing" (James 1:4) for the fulfillment of this lifelong endeavor. Let patience work within you contentment and wholesomeness so that your preordained mate will find you, "entire and wanting nothing" (James 1:4).

15 Spirit of Loneliness

Fifthly, let's share reasons why we, as singles, experience anxiety concerning marriage. Oftentimes, during this discovery period, the spirit of loneliness tightly grips our soul. We respond to the spirit of loneliness with despair, agony, desperation, dejection, despondence and discouragement. We allow the spirit of loneliness to abide in our lives with such stronghold that we ache and cry out as one in the wilderness who will never be found.

Singles, reactive positively to the spirit of loneliness. Utilize this critical preparatory process to become wholesome. Become proactive and strive daily to fulfill the commandments in the scriptures. Take the double cross away from the adversary and admit that you are alone. When you take the double cross away from the adversary and admit you are alone, then the spirit of loneliness has no place to root. Furthermore, choose to look positive at the state of loneliness. There is a major difference in being alone and being lonely.

Alone is a positive state of oneness or independence. Lonely is a negative state of emptiness in self or lonesome. Alone is more of an external state whereas lonely is more of an internal state. Alone is without the physical companion of another, human, while lonely is void of internal companion of the Holy Spirit, the Comforter. Alone means incomparable and unique; it implies individuality, entireness, solemnness, exclusiveness and independence. Lonely means sad from being cut off from others or friendliness; it implies desolation, seclusion, isolation and bleakness. Choose to look at the "state of being alone" as a positive state of singleness, completeness, fulfillment, solitary and celibacy. Realize that the spirit of loneliness is a state of barrenness, withdrawn, rejection, and god-forsaken.

Remember, Jesus' word before He ascended to heaven. Jesus said, I will not leave you comfortless. But I will send you a Comforter, the Holy Spirit, to abide with you and in you. The Comforter when abiding in one, provides the individuality, entireness, solemnness, exclusiveness, independence, completeness and fulfillment.

Be cognizant that during this waiting period, we should focus on the positive side of singleness. Realize, there are advantages to singleness (which will be discussed in Part Five). Focus less on finding or being discovered by our mate and more on finding peace and contentment by discovering our purpose in Jesus. Yes, the adversary causes us to feel isolated and segregated from the club of marriage, detached from society and separated from our rib.

Singles, the adversary's job is to seek whom he may

devour. The adversary is doing his job by seeking and devouring you with the spirit of loneliness. Why not counteract the devil's spirit of loneliness by taking away the double cross from the devil and do your job. Christians, we must be about our father's business. Continue to let patience have her perfect work (James 1:4a) until God orchestrates the two of you to meet.

A paradigm shift must occur during this state of singleness. Allow the Holy Spirit to transform and renew our mind with the mind of Christ. Conform to a life of holiness and become heavenly minded. Our discourse must communicate thoughts of pureness, holiness and of good reports. Admit you are single; but, you and Christ are one. Thank God for your singleness and the time singleness affords which is to take the yoke of Jesus and learn of Him. Fall in love with being single.

Make your request known unto God concerning what you want and need and not of what you don't have or need during this period of singleness (Philippians 4:6). Remember to be careful for nothing; pray about everything concerning your life. Give thanksgiving and praise to God for all his blessings. I am confidence when you apply the above scriptures to your life, you won't be single much longer. Contemplate these scriptures.

5:14-15 This is the confidence that we have in Him: that if we ask anything according to His will, he heareth us: And if we know that he hear us, whatsoever we ask, we know that we have the petitions that we desired of him (I John).

Dr. Gale Cook Shumaker

PART FIVE

16 Single and Fulfilled

. . . singleness, a gift from God (I Corinthians 7:7-8).

Allow me to detour a few pages to share a nugget or two from Apostle Paul's teaching in Corinthians Seventh Chapter. Apostle Paul's ministry in Corinth, consisted of teaching about the lifestyle of the married and unmarried. Paul has such powerful instructions on living a pure and chaste life. He spoke to the virgins about purity and chastity. He outlined the duties of an unmarried person. He compared a human's body to a temple. He spoke to the married about their duties and responsibilities to their husband and to the Lord. He offered advice to persons who were once married and who are widowed or divorced.

Paul had a personal desire and preference toward the institution of marriage. Paul's preference was to remain unmarried; he celebrated his singleness. He found contentment and fulfillment in the single lifestyle that he chose. In my opinion, Apostle Paul found the key to living a single and fulfilled lifestyle. He conveyed confidence in being available to give himself whole heartedly and uncompromisingly to God's kingdom work. He understood the importance of sharing a life of singleness to fulfil the mission of Jesus Christ.

As I read about the devoted single life of handmaiden Kathryn Kuhnman and as I reflect on my own life before and after marriage, I understand the power and advantages of being unmarried, "singleness." One can experience an undivided, complete devotion and loyalty to God. One is without carefulness to the things of the world (I Corinthians 7:32), but with complete carefulness to the things of God.

Below is Table One that shows the unmarried and the married duties and responsibilities. This Table summarizes Apostle Paul's teaching of I Corinthians 6 and 7 chapters.

Table One: Duties and Responsibilities of the Unmarried and Married

Unmarried	Married
1. Body belongs to God (I Cor. 6:19)	1. Body belongs to spouse (I Cor. 7:4)
2.Care for the things of God (I Cor. 7:32)	2. Care for the things of world (I Cor. 7:33)
3. Pleases God (I Cor. 7:32)	3. Pleases spouse (I Cor. 7:33)

Below is Table Two that shows the contrast of the church and wife. This table summarizes the duties and responsibilities of the church and wife extracted from 1 Corinthians chapter 6 and 7.

Table Two: Duties and Responsibilities of the Church and Wife

Church	Wife
1.Glorifies God with body/spirit (I Cor 6:20).	1. Render due benevolence to spouse (ICor. 7:3).
2. Join to Lord in one spirit (I Cor. 6:17))	2. Care for the things of world (I Cor. 7:33)
3. Pleases God (I Cor. 7:32)	3. Join to spouse in one (I Cor. 6:16)

Further, Apostle Paul stated that, "he would that all men would remain unmarried like himself. " He further stated that it would be good for the unmarried, the widows and the divorced (I Corinthians 7:8 and 27) to abide like him. However, he realized that the ability to remain single and pure was a gift from God (I Corinthians 7:7-8).

Paul understood that all Christians were not called to live a single life. He knew that one had to possess the gift, the special qualities and capabilities to remain single. Apostle Paul statement to Christians were to "abide with God in the calling in which we are called (I Corinthians 7:20 and 24). Yet, Paul said if you can't abstain marry (7:2).

17 Needful Things

As I struggled with the decision to marry or not to marry, I contemplated that the essential and minimal scriptural requirements were not met concerning being equally yoked as Christians. The desire was present in my heart to marry but the questions that needed answering were: "Is God granting His perfect will for my desire to be fulfilled?" "Is this the season for marriage?"

Singles, until Jesus grants His perfect will and the desires of our heart concerning a mate, we must continue to seek the needful things of God. We must:

1. Hide ourselves in the Lord, performing our Father's business. In this hidden state, we must study the Word of God to show ourselves approved unto God as a workmen that is not ashamed to rightly dividing the Word of truth (II Timothy 2:15). Then, and only, are we prepared to put on the whole armor of God, that we may be able to stand against all the wiles of the devil's temptations (Ephesians 6:11).

2. Continue to pray without ceasing (I Thessalonians 5:17). Further, we must become spiritual receptacles or vessels and thereby, utilize

this time to pray and receive all the sweet pillow talk that Jesus wants to utter during prayer time. We then, must rely on this spiritual relationship as a pillar of strength to sustain us in our weakest hours of temptation.

3. Labor in the vineyard performing God's will and fulfilling our purpose. More importantly, we must remain faithful and busy, witnessing and winning souls for Christ and the kingdom. We must witness to persons in our neighborhoods (Jerusalem), in our state (Judea), in all states (Samaria) and in all nations (uttermost part of the world) (Acts 1:8). We must "lose" ourselves in Jesus' kingdom work in order that we can be "found" by the preordained mate.

4. Involved oneself in an intimate relationship with the Lord through worship. Moreover, develop your spiritual man through prayer and meditation to the Lord. We must bask in the Lord's presence so that we may experience the richness of "green pastures," the peace of "still waters" and the freshness of a "restored soul" (Psalms 23).

5. Care for the "needful things" concerning the Lord and care to please Him in all affairs. Paul

proclaimed, "He who is unmarried cares for the things that belong to the Lord, how he may please the Lord" (I Corinthian 7:32). Singles, I challenge each of you to please Jesus as Mary did; Mary anointed the Lord with ointment, humbly wiped His feet with her glory, her mane (Saint John 12:3) and sat at Jesus' feet to hear the Word (Saint Luke 10:39). We cannot afford the time or energy to be sidetracked with the cares and habits of the world as did Martha, the sister of Mary and Lazarus of Bethany (Saint Luke 10:40-42).

40-But Martha was cumbered about much serving, and came to him, and said, Lord, dost thou not care that my sister hath left me to serve alone? Bid her therefore that she help me.

41-And Jesus answered and said unto her, Martha, Martha, thou art careful and troubled about many things:

42-But one thing is needful: and Mary hath chosen that good part, which shall not be taken away from her (KJV). Selah.

Ladies and gentlemen, when we do what the scripture outlines as a prerequisite, "the needful thing, that good part," we are setting the stage to be found by the ordained husband through the Holy Spirit's orchestration. Further, we are choosing that "good part" which shall not be taken away from us (Saint Luke 10:42b).

6. Be holy both in body and spirit as the scripture commanded. Let's ponder Paul's address in First Corinthians. Paul stated that, "the unmarried woman cares for the things of the Lord, that she may be holy both in body and in spirit" (7:34b). Paul says:

What? Know ye not that your body is the temple of the Holy Ghost which is in you, which ye have of God, and ye are not your own? 1Corinthians 3:15-16

For ye are bought with a price: therefore glorify God in your body, and in your spirit, which are God's. I Corinthians 6:20.

18 Body and Spirit

Apostle Paul is very adamant about his perception of the duties of an unmarried person. Paul's discourse is communicated with such clarity that little room is left for error or misunderstandings in this era of errors. He outlines specific and detailed instructions and knowledge for the unmarried.

In the above scriptural passage, Paul gives very powerful and life-changing reasons why women are to be holy in body and spirit.

(1) ". . . And ye are not your own?" In this scripture, Apostle Paul makes a statement and asks a question simultaneously (I Corinthians 6:19b). Ownership is questioned in this verse as he asks and tells you a powerful fact. Hear the voice and conviction of Paul as He says: (a) "You are not your own," and; (b) Do you know that you are not you own? Paul answers the question and provide information to support the statement in the same verse. He answers, ". . . ye have of God" (6:19) and ". . . which are God's" 7:20). Other words, Paul stated that our body belongs to God.

(2) ". . . Your body is the temple of the Holy Ghost." Apostle Paul makes a statement that our body is the temple

of the Holy Spirit which is in you. In essence, the temple is to be utilized for the indwelling place of the Holy Spirit. The body as the temple (I Corinthians 6:18), is a house, a home, a dwelling place, where the Holy Spirit resides. The Holy Spirit is the Spirit which came after Jesus' ascension and which one receives of or from God.

(3) "For ye are bought with a price." Apostle Paul outlines the underlining concept of ownership in I Corinthians 6:20a. This passage establishes ownership, the buyer and cost of ownership. Paul points out in I Corinthians 6:20, that God paid a price for our body. When a purchase is made by a consumer, there is a general need for or alike of the property purchased. However, God, the purchaser, not only needed or liked mankind, "God so loved the world, that He gave His only begotten Son, the price, (Saint John 3:16) as a ransom for mankind.

19 God's Things

In essence, this passage clearly states that we, our body (the house, the home and dwelling place of the Holy Spirit), are bought with a price. Subsequently, you did not purchased yourself; we are owned, purchased by and belong to God. This passage also states that not only do the body (faculty, figure, frame and form) belongs to Christ; but, the spirit (life, heart, soul) also belongs to God.

(4) ". . . Therefore glorify God in your body and spirit which are God". The lesson in this passage is to glorify (magnify, worship, idolize and honor) God in your body and spirit which are both God's. God purchased our body for a dwelling place for the Holy Spirit. Then He gifted us with the Holy Spirit, the Comforter and Promise which leads, teaches, guides and brings all things back to one's remembrance. For the aforementioned purpose, it is imperative to receive the gift of the Holy Spirit that was promised to comfort us in a time of need.

To glorify God in your body and spirit, one is to celebrate, commemorate, enshrine and reverence the Creator, Purchaser and Giver of the body and spirit. To glorify God in your body implies keeping the body pure and clean for the indwelling of the Holy Spirit. To glorify God in your spirit, implies cultivating a perpetual praise, worship, and thanksgiving spirit, expressing exaltation, edification and graciousness to God. Paul says:

(a) ". . . Therefore glorify God in your body . . . which are [is] God". We are encourage to glorify God in your body which is the physical structure that encases our spirit and soul. It is the matter that one sees when looking at a being.

(b) ". . . Therefore glorify God in your spirit . . . which are [is] God". We are encouraged to glorify God in your spirit, the sheer essence of our being. The spirit refers to the intuition, instinctive and cognitive part of us that know things from, about and of God.

(c) It was established earlier on that the unmarried woman cares for the "things" of the Lord. These things are the "body" and the "spirit". We know that the unmarried cares to keep her borrowed body and spirit, holy, because they actually belong to God. Thus, we are to glorify God in our body and spirit or rather His body and spirit that He, God, has allowed us to utilize as humans.

20 Good Things

Moreover, we are to flee sexual immorality, fornication (I Corinthians 6:17-19) and adultery (Proverbs 6:32). Fornication is sexual intimacy that is committed by two unmarried people. Adultery is sexual intimacy involving at least one married person. Fornication is heavily emphasized over adultery because an unmarried person should be (1) pure and chaste until marriage, and (2) experiencing an intimacy relationship with God, caring and pleasing God; whereas in adultery, a married person should be (1) intimate already and with only her/his spouse, and (2) caring and pleasing his/her mate foremost. However, one is to flee both fornication and adultery.

Fornication is sexual intimacy against, the temple of the Holy Spirit. Fornication is sin against your body, like blasphemy is sin against the Holy Spirit. When Paul says "flee fornication", God is not trying to withhold any good thing from you. For "no good thing will He withhold from those who walk uprightly" (Psalms 84:11). Sexual intimacy is one of the good things and benefit reserved for the married ones. It is the mean in which a man and woman consummate a marriage and become one, produce children and replenish the earth. However, God purpose sexual intimacy to benefit a married couple, namely, a man and woman. Remember, scripture says, "he who finds a wife, finds a good thing" (Proverb).

Now, the scripture has plainly stated the course of action for the unmarried people. Paul stated that, "the unmarried woman cares for the things of the Lord, how she may please Him" (7:34). So singles purpose to please God during your unmarried life. Then, you will be equipped with the knowledge and skills, not experience, on how to please your master and lord, husband during your married life. In essence, develop the appropriate relationship during the ripe time.

21 Lifestyle

The scripture sanctions virginity or abstinence which means being holy in the body. Further, the scripture sanction sexual and moral purity which means being holy in the body, mind and spirit. Therefore, celibacy must become a lifestyle. Celibacy, sexual and moral purity must become a lifestyle.

Now, Paul speaks expressively to you, the woman and man who have been married (I Corinthians 7:27). Paul states, ". . . . If thou marry, thou hast not sinned. If a virgin marry, she hath not sinned. Nevertheless, such shall have trouble in the flesh: but I spare you (I Corinthians 7:28). In this passage, Paul admonishes the woman, widow and the divorced, that she will encounter trouble in the flesh. At one time, a widow and a divorced woman's attention was diverted from pleasing the Lord and fulfilling the care of the Lord ultimately, to pleasing her husband and fulfilling the passion of marriage. Subsequently, the passion of marriage has become banal, commonplace, and the act of marriage is familiar. One will have trouble when an acquired appetite is not fulfilled, i.e., the passion of marriage and abstaining from the said passion.

Paul concludes this issue when he stated, "But this I say, brethren, the time is short. It remains, that they who have wives should be as though they have none (I Corinthians 7:29). The Lord is requiring that we remain sober, and watchful unto prayer for the end of all things is at hand (I Peter 4:7). He is encouraging us to focus on pleasing the Lord, regardless, of our marriage state.

Yes, it happened to me. For I chose a seed and waited not for the creation and full development of the tree, the preordained husband that My Adonai prepared for me. I heard God's gentle voice when he said, a "greater one shall come." However, at that point, I had committed; I was in dire need for the Lord to bail me out of this one. For once in my life, I was so ashamed of my mistake. When I sat in God's presence at my special prayer time, all I could do was to weep in his presence because of my mistake.

No, I did not heed to God's directions on this request. I was miserable. Nonetheless, I waved with the tides and kept my commitment that I made before man and God. In spite of the abuse I endured, I endeavor to keep my vows. I was too ashamed to pray for God's intervention. The war and battles that I encountered in the marriage were unfamiliar to me, but not my Master, my Adonai. For God wage war, fought battles and won.

"I know the devil and the devil knows me!

I breathe God; for it was God who blew life back into me.

I feast on God, as I meditate on His Word day and night.

I live for God, dwelling in the house of God:

Inquiring about His secrets and mysteries that are made known only to a few, His called, chosen, and elected ones."

PART SIX
22 Soulmate
"they shall be one" (Genesis 2:24) .

After much prayer and fasting, I consented and married, conceivably my soulmate. I made the determination too married. It was my volition to marry; however, I must admit once again that it was not a sober decision. For it was quite the contrary; it was an intoxicated decision.

My Tree, my soulmate, communicated that his expectations of a husband were parallel to the scripture (Ephesians 5:23, 28 and Colossians 3:19). Although he communicated that he fulfilled the commands delineated by the scripture concerning a husband, the behavior exhibited by my mate was not aligned with the scripture or with what he communicated. The behavior that my soulmate exhibited was not the behavior of one who is a soulmate nor of one who is equally yoked with another Christian in biblical beliefs.

A soulmate being a compound word, has a compound meaning. The soul in soulmate is the essence, substance, or actuating cause of life (Webster Dictionary). Soul, in many instances refers to one's vitality, character, identity, force, mind and heart. The Greek word for soul, "zoe or zao", means "life or life-giving" (Strong, 1996). The mate of soulmate is a comrade, a husband or wife, man or woman, and a suitable companion (Webster Dictionary). A mate is one who complements, consorts, copulates, connects, consolidates, correlates and combines with a counterpart. A soulmate is a companion, a comrade who is joined together or combine with another in will, emotion and mind for the duration of their lives. Soulmates take on the vitality, characteristics and identification of each other and act, react and proact as two united as one.

Now, a soulmate assists and loves his mate through all crises whether "good or bad times, sickness or healthiness, richness or poorness or until the last enemy, death, visits." A soulmate vows to a lifelong commitment as he unites as one with his mate. True soulmates will be equally yoked in as many areas of their existence, (soulical [mind, emotion and will] and spiritual [conscience, intuition and worship]) as possible in order that the devil will not have the invitation to double cross the couple. The specific areas in which the couple isn't equally yoke, will be the chosen areas in which the devil will wage war in their marriage and double cross the couple. The double cross usually occur in an area in which the soulmates disagree unremittingly. However, there is sacred and inherent power in the "two" touching, agreeing and binding the devil from activities within the marriage.

A true soulmate's relationship occurs and exists when two persons, specifically man and woman, are created and refined explicitly and suitably for each other in all realms of existence: bodily, soulically and spiritually. When a man finds a wife, his good thing, the man and woman become one and unite, soulically, through sharing wedding vows, spiritually, through commitment and fulfillment of the vows, and physically, through consummation.

In Genesis 2:21-22, the Lord God took one of Adam's ribs and made a woman and presented the woman, Eve unto Adam. This scripture clearly depicts that God purposely made Eve for Adam. As God intentionally made Eve for Adam, so will God create a woman explicitly and suitably for the man who stays completely in God's divine will as Adam was before the fall of man. The scripture also depicts that God provided Adam with all that he needed in the form of a helpmate, Eve.

The Lord, God, loved Adam so much until He not only made a woman, Eve, explicitly and suitably for Adam, the Lord God also created the woman from Adam's rib and presented the woman, Eve, unto Adam. God gave Adam his helpmeet on a silver platter in the Garden of Eden. Adam did not have to "find or look for his good thing". For Adam was blessed and highly favor; therefore, God blessed Adam with his helpmeet and soulmate.

Today, man has to "find, look, hunt for and then closely observe, pray and choose "his good things" or wife. Oftentimes, man finds and settles for a wife who is not explicitly and suitably created for his specific needs, purpose and mission. On the other hand, the woman too often, settles for a man who was not ordained as her husband; therefore, the needs of both man and woman are not met in a marriage.

Further, what a couple has to contemplate before and during marriage is that the needs and challenges of a marriage change as the two persons enter and exit many different transitional periods in life. As the couple matures from newlyweds to parents to grandparents so are there many changes and challenges. The needs and challenges change from sheer sexual intimacy and provision, to companionship and support, and finally to that of fulfilment and the comfort zone. The challenges change from career development to home selection to investment. The needs and challenges change from birthing an infant(s) and caring for a family to educating and marrying of the children to empty-nesting and retirement.

The transitional periods in a marriage will finally

become the measuring stick as to whether or not a couple is a soulmate. When one weathers the storms of a marriage and faces the needs and challenges of a marriage in progress, then can the two declare that they are soulmate. It will then be appropriate to say, the "twain is indeed one."

23 Spiritual Marriage

After I married my tree, my soulmate, a pastor of a church, doubt and fear gripped the essence of my soul as I uttered "I do". I became so attuned spiritually to what God meant in Genesis, "the twain shall become one". However, I knew that we would never become one as the scripture stated. For one, I knew that if the two were to become one, the couple must have as a foundation, all that the scriptures outlined i.e., and the love explained in I Corinthians 13:4-7.

The "I Corinthians 13 love" is one that "suffers long and is kind." This love envies not, vaunts not, nor puffs not. Further, love behaves itself seemly, seeketh not her own, not easily provoked and thinks no evil. This love rejoices not in iniquity but rejoices in the truth. True love bears, believes, hopes and endures all things. In essence, this love, describes the agape love, spontaneous, divine and eternal. It is one in which a mate displays patience, kindness, generosity, courtesy, unselfishness, good temperament, righteousness and sincerity toward another.

I knew that I made a lifelong vow that encompassed a lifelong commitment of working toward "becoming one". I knew that I vowed for the duration of my life. I took this promise so personal and sacred until I reorganized my priorities and placed as goal one, "becoming one" with the person I united in holy matrimony.

Secondly, if I were to become one with my mate, equal yoked is a concept that must be considered. This oneness referenced is not just the physical oneness that occurs during the consummation process, this oneness is what divinely occurs when two becomes one spiritually. This is a spiritual oneness that occurs with the indwelling of the Holy Spirit.

Think for a moment. Is it humanly possible for one human with all their flaws, shortcomings and sinful nature to actually "become one" with another human with perhaps, with a different set of flaws and shortcomings and sinful nature? Did Adam and Eve actually become one? Were they soulmates? Did Adam and Eve remain in a state of oneness? Although Adam and Eve started their life as one in body, were they actually one soulically, in living? Were they one spiritually? Were Adam and Eve separated soulically before becoming one spiritually? Did not Eve walk and listen to the serpent while Adam walked and listened to the Lord? It is spiritual possible for a human with all their flaws, shortcomings and their sinful nature to actually "become one" with another human with perhaps, a different set of flaws and shortcomings and sinfully nature, it is spiritually possible?

24 They Shall Become One

At the beginning of May of 1997, on one stormy night, my husband and I departed for the last time. In my spirit, I knew this was final. So as he packed, I went to the room where he was gathering his belongings. Twice, I asked him did he want to reconsider. The Holy Spirit said ask him a third time. I said, "He will think I am begging him." I asked him a third time to reconsider. He replied, "stop begging me.' I laughed until I cried. You see, "begging" is not my choice word. I was being obedience to God in asking a third time. He looked at me as if I had lost my mind. When he pulled out the driveway, the Holy Spirit silently said, "It's finished."

On the weekend after his departure and as I walked through the yard picking up small bits of paper and other debris that the storm had blown into my yard, I noticed pieces of dollar bills that were all torn and worn into many pieces. The bills were disfigured, wrinkled and dried. They had dried with dirt and layers of mud all in the folds. They had been soaked over and over again in many of nature's elements. The bills had gone through many changes. I hesitantly picked up the many pieces, hurriedly took them inside and gently place them on the small breakfast table. I was encouraged by the indwelling of the Holy Spirit to put the pieces of bills together. The Lord ministered to the essence of my life as I formed whole dollar from the pieces. There were two, one dollar bills: one bill was torn in four pieces; the other bill was torn into six pieces. As I placed the pieces in the correct place, to form a whole bill, the Holy Spirit quietly whispered, these bills are symbolic of your marriage. These bills are representative of the many vicissitudes that you all encountered during this marriage. With the one dollar bill that was torn into six parts, two small portions were missing. I humored and thought, God, am I representative of the four-piece bill or the six-piece bill?

The two whole persons whom God had allowed to become twain, were once again two persons. However, we were not two whole persons. We were two broken persons who had gone through the storm of a marriage. We had been tossed, disfigured and wrinkled because of the storm of life. We had been worn and broken into many pieces as the two, one dollar bills that I found. Although the two dollar bills were spendable, one would have to tape the bills together to form whole bills in order to use them as currency. I pondered, only God, himself, could heal such brokenness that the two could circulate into society in a wholesome state.

At this juncture, I realized that Jesus bored many stripes and bruises for the healing that is desperately needed for this brokenness.   However, a small stilled voice quietly said, look on the back of these bills. It had printed on them, "In God We Trust."   "Always remember, "In God We Trust". Never forget to put your trust in me. Receive your healing for your brokenness."

The bills depicted the brokenness of our heart and spirit. The Lord is near those who have a broke spirit and save those who have a contrite heart (Psalms 34:18). A broke heart is the sacrifices of God; furthermore, God will not despise a broken and a contrite heart (Psalms 51:17). Also, God heals the broken hearted and binds up there wounds (Psalms 147:13).

Further, the disfigured, wrinkled and dried bills that were found torn in many pieces in the yard were symbolic of how caring for the things of this world can draw one off the spiritual course and mission to a chaotic and fruitless end. The story of Mary, Martha and Lazarus is very helpful toward understanding about the cares of this world.

The many changes that the bills had undergone in the midst of the stormy weather is parallel to the many harsh transitions that one encounters when living outside the perfect and divine will of God the Father. Picking up the many pieces of money, hurriedly taking the pieces inside, and gently placing them on the small breakfast table is the norm of how Jesus reacts and handle our crises. Jesus hastily comes to our rescue and immediately heals us and makes us whole.

25 Marriage is Spiritual

Marriage is more than just a bodily and soulical action. A true marriage is spiritual. The success and longevity of a marriage are contingent on a couple being one in the spirit with the Spiritual One, the Godhead. A man and a woman must be spiritually and equally yoked with the Spiritual One to have a successful marriage. So it is with the body of Christ, the church, which must become one and united in character, without spot, wrinkle and blemish, prior to Jesus' return to marry his bride. When a husband and wife unite in a marriage, they fulfil the mission that God purposed for a man and woman.

How could a couple fail effortlessly in a marriage and yet, work so very diligently to become a part of Jesus' wedding party? How could a couple fall effortlessly in their earthly marriage and strive earnestly to become a part of the heavenly marriage? Does Scripture say, "He who is faithful in little (earthly marriage) will be faithful in much" (heavenly marriage)? Does scripture say that the two shall be one (Genesis 2:24)? Could this mean that the husband and wife must become one body on earth? Does this mean that the husband-wife oneness on earth unites with other husbands and wives teams and families to become the one CHURCH, the one BODY, and the one BRIDE, which Jesus will return to marry? Do we see the picture as Jesus intended? Do we fulfill the mission of marriage as Jesus purposed? Would Jesus say well done good and faith servant as a judgment on marriage? Selah.

PART SEVEN
26 Pastor, First Lady, and The Church
Introduction

. . . And he is the head of the body, the church (Colossians 1:18) or " the church of God" (Acts 20:28).

Part Seven of this book is very crucial for the pastors, first ladies and churches and their roles in fulfilling the scripture. An effort is made to share the vision of the original and true "CHURCH of GOD." The vision of the "Church of God" is laid out according to Apostles Paul and Peter in Acts 20:28, Ephesians 5:23-33 and I Peter 5:1-4. A detailed discussion [and the history] of the Church of God will be cited later in this segment.

An effort is made in this book to bridge the gap between what God purposed ministers to preach with how Jesus fulfilled and lived what was preached, the Word. Further, an effort is made to discuss how the Gospel, Principles and Doctrine of Jesus Christ should be implemented into daily living and practices. In other words, an effort is made to connect the Doctrine of Jesus Christ with practical principles so that one may live a holy lifestyle which would serve to usher in the kingdom that is to come. Jesus lived the Word, became the Word and was (is) the Word;

therefore, if He fulfilled the Word, so can we. Remember, and greater things shall we do, if and when we believe.

Oftentimes, one may find that the principles and truths of the bible are taught; but, the ways, methods, and daily practices of fulfilling those principles and truths are not taught. The message is thoroughly proclaimed; but, the method is not merely explained. Even when the principles and the truth are taught and practiced, Christians still struggle with maintaining a Christian lifestyle. It appears that the temptation to live unholy is more enticing than the daily rewards to live holy. It seems that one lives holy daily only to receive the crown of life after death.

However, when one relaxes and experience the fullness of joy, pleasures evermore and the peace that surpasses all understanding, one can then, experience and enjoy daily rewards for living holy. Christians take issues with the concept of being rooted and sealed by the Holy Spirit in this Christian walk. Christians are yet to grasp the "power of choice" concerning living a Christian and holy lifestyle. "Holiness without, no man shall see the Lord" (Hebrew 12:14)." Choose this day whom you will serve. I say, choose this day, how you will live.

Part Seven of this book which reveals the vision of the true "Church of God," may be simple and familiar. However, the revelation knowledge and the uncompromising truth inherited within this section of the manuscript are critical to the success, glory and victory of the church and the kingdom to come. "All, everything, hinges on the revelation inherited in these few pages", said the Holy Spirit. Paul stated, "For this is a great mystery . . . concerning Christ and the church" (Ephesians 5:32). What is this great mystery? Well, the essence of the mystery of Christ and the church is being shared through this piece of literature to the followers of Christ

Pastor's First Ladies and Churches

The title and the concept of this book originated from this section. This book, as the title suggests, addresses interrelationships between pastors, pastors' spouses, church members and the church from an earthly and a spiritually perspectives. The relationships and interrelationships are illustrations of activities that exist within modern day churches. The relationships that exist within churches should represent the Gospel of Jesus Christ and should follow the examples that the Lord modeled through the life of Jesus Christ.

The content of this book was undoubtedly inspired by the Holy Spirit. As I typed the information that the Holy Spirit wanted to share with His people, THE WORD, the words, rolled out of my spirit as water runs from a faucet. I cannot type fast enough for Him. Although, I feel so inadequate to be chosen to write this in-time, rama and prophetic word, I feel so renewed and refreshed as Christ imparts this vision and mystery unto me. I feel so inadequate to the Holy Spirit's brilliance; yet, I feel so at peace, so perfect and unified with Him as He imparts to me and I into you, this revelation knowledge.

As I write, the Holy Spirit baptizes me so intensely. Tears cloud my vision as He reveals the true vision of the Church. As I write, I am constantly and steadfastly emerged in the still waters and the great anointing as He, the Lord, restores my soul. In the submerging and the restoring processes, the Lord healed me of many illnesses and diseases that encamped my body and that I was not cognizant of having. He flushed my body of all infirmities that many people have to pay their life's earnings to acquire medical treatments and healing; some have to pay the cost of their very life.

Why this section of the book became Part Seven only the Holy Spirit truly knows. The spiritual symbolism of the number "seven" is perfection. However, the Holy Spirit's expectation of Pastors, First Ladies and the Churches, is to go from grace to grace and to grow from grace to perfection. Our roles, pastor, first lady and the church, must be viewed from the spiritual perspective. We should execute those roles and duties with such vigor and vim as our life, our eternal life, depends on it. Our lives do indeed depend on getting it right this time. We should become spiritually in tuned so that we may receive revelation knowledge and guidance on how to lead our churches and people to victory. For victory in Jesus is victory for Jesus.

Further, we must not become overly zealous in the matter of fulfilling the vision for the Church of God that we step outside the guidance of the Holy Spirit and the will of Jesus Christ. We must certainly not reinvent that which God has divinely invented and created as a guiding light for our fulfillment and purpose. The wheel, the plan of salvation, and the strategies to fulfil the original vision for the Church of God have been invented. We, must therefore, roll with the wheel, the plan, the vision, the mystery, as we unroll the scroll that holds the sacred strategies and principles for the Pastors, First Ladies and Churches.

We must diligently seek knowledge and understand concerning this sacred plan, great mystery and vision. Further, we must reach the goal that we were created to fulfil. Pastors, First Ladies and Churches, must strive with the essence of our might to reach our destiny. Finally, let patience have her perfect work, so that at the end times, we, THE CHURCH, will be perfect, entire, holy, glorious, and without spot, wrinkle, blemish and in want of nothing (James 1:4 and Ephesians 5:25-27).

Vision, Blueprints of Victory

The vision for the church of God originated before the foundation of the world. This vision is simple. It is given to sustain man and the church. It provides direction and purpose. For without the vision, man would surely perish (Proverb 29:18). Without the vision man would surely be lost in the wilderness. Without fulfillment of the vision, man and his existence will become a wilderness.

Apostle Paul and Peter encourage the pastors to implement the vision for the church of God. The vision for the church of God is a shared vision. It is the vision that all churches must implement. The components of the vision are essentially ground-building beliefs, foundational principles and pillars of strengths that encase the blueprints of victory for the true church of God. These components must always be the focus of the spiritual leaders.

When this vision is accomplished by all pastors, overseers, bishops and elders at their respective churches, then, will the ultimate purpose and destiny of all churches be fulfilled? That ultimate purpose is the unification of all churches to create "the Church of God." Henceforth, the ultimate purpose for pastors is to present to Christ a "glorious church, which is without a spot, wrinkle or any such thing.' Furthermore, this "glorious church should be holy and without blemish" (Ephesians 5:27).

The churches that do not fulfilled this vision, will be liken unto the five foolish virgins who did not have oil in their lamps when the bridge groom came or the servant who received one talent and hid the one talent, money, in the earth. However, the churches that do fulfilled the vision of the church of God will be liken unto the five wise virgins who had oil in their vessels or the servant who received five talents, traded those five talents and received five more talents (Saint Matthew 25).

The churches that do receive and implement the vision of God will be received by Christ, the bridegroom, as a part of His kingdom. However, the churches that do not receive nor implement the vision will be left behind when the bridegroom comes. Those churches that share the vision of God will increase their talents as well as function as God ordained His churches to function. Further, the churches of God that fulfill the vision will unify to become the one great big and only "glorious' Church of God" when Jesus returns.

The vision for the church of God is calling for all pastors to be faithful in the portion that God called them to do. Henceforth, Apostle Peter is saying, take this vision, this oversight, and study and inspect it; become responsible for fulfilling this duty, vision and mission statement. However, if and when the pastors, shepherds and overseers align and implement the vision for their church with the vision for the church of God, then and only then, is the vision in part accomplished for "the Church of God." Nonetheless, the vision for every true Church of God that is currently operating according to Acts 20:28 and I Peter 5:2-4, must be aligned with the vision for the Church of God. When this occurs, the pastors are fulfilling their divine purpose for existing. They are fulfilling their destiny. Further, Pastors are thereby doing kingdom work, preparing the kingdom that is to come. Ultimately, the pastors are accomplishing the vision of the church of God.

Vision For The Church

"Mission Statement"

In the Books of Acts and I Peter, Apostles Paul and Peter offered a prophetic word to pastors, bishops, elders and overseers in the biblical times which is applicable to pastors of today. In this scripture, hinges many biblical truths that are evident. Apostle Peter says,

> 5:1 "The elders which are among you I exhort, who am also an elder, and a witness of the sufferings of Christ, and also a partaker of the glory that shall be

revealed:"

5:2 "Feed the flock of God which is among you, taking the oversight thereof, not by constraint, but willingly; and not for filthy lucre, but of a ready mind" (I Peter).

This word of wisdom in this passage is spoken by Peter, an Elder, Apostle, a servant, witness and partaker, and is spoken expressively to bishops, pastors, elders and overseers of churches (I Peter 5:1). Peter denotes his spiritual experiences and authority as a laborer of Christ as he spoke adamantly concerning the admonition and vision of God for the Church.

In this vision and prophetic word, Apostle Peter not only admonishes overseers, he also advises, counsels, instructs, impels and cautions the pastors, bishops, elders, and the overseers to "feed the flock of God which is among you" (I Peter 5:2). This prophetic word outlines the first component of the vision for the church of God, yesterday, today and tomorrow.

The Flock of God

The flock, tsone (Hebrew), pomimnion (Greek), means multitude and crowd. The "flock of God" denotes that sheep are led by a shepherd. Metaphorically, the "flock of

God," denotes churches that are cared for by pastors, bishops, elders and overseers (Acts 20:28; and, I Peter 5:1-4). The "flock of God," metaphorically, is Christ's followers (Saint Matthew 26:31; Saint Luke 2:8; and I Corinthians 9:7) and Christ's disciples (Saint Luke 12:32). Furthermore, it symbolizes Christians of many churches which are also inclusive of the pastors, bishops, elders and overseers (Vines, 1970). In essence, the "flock of God" is the Christians who know the voice of God, the chief shepherd, and who hearken, listen and obey His commands, his teaching, his words (Saint John 10:14-16).

Now, this prophetic vision and mission statement say, "feed the flock of God which is among you." Apostle Peter is referencing the Christians who are in the congregation that the pastor oversees. Apostle Peter is admonishing the pastors to feed the flock which is in the midst of, surrounded by, in the company of, associated with the church he/she oversees.

In laymen terms, Apostle Paul directs this vision towards the "flock of God which is among you." This flock includes many types and groups of people who fellowship at the church. The "flock of God" encompasses "the Greeks, the Barbarians, the Romans, the wise and the unwise," (Romans 1:14). Apostle Paul exclaims, feed the civilized, the uncivilized, the learned, the unlearned, the scholars, the intelligent and the unintelligent, all who are among you. Paul states, ". . . . I am ready to preach the gospel to 'all of' you 'and to those' that are at Rome also" (Romans 1:15). This passage is inclusive of all who make up the flock, the body of the church of God.

First Component of the Vision and Mission Statement

Apostle Peter also in this prophetic passage and vision to pastors outlined not only the principles and truths of this vision, but the ways and methods of fulfilling this vision. Peter's message proclaims, "Feed the flock of God which is among you;" then, he explains the method, the what(s) an how(s).

What to Feed the Flock

Apostle Peter says implement this vision for the church of God willingly, freely, eagerly, readily, and graciously and without constraint, restriction, intimidation, control, force, and reservation. He advocates in this passage to pastors, bishops, elders and overseers, will to do God's meat that you were pre- and ordained to do. Complete the mission, the vision, the work in which you were sent to accomplish (Saint John 4:34). Feed the flock the Word, the word of God and the truth.

The vision for the church of God is calling for all

pastors to be faithful in the portion that God called them to do. For the vision states, "take the oversight thereof, not by constraint, but willingly; and not for filthy lucre, but of a ready mind" (I Peter 5:2-3)." In this passage, Apostle Peter is advising pastors to "look upon, look at, exercise oversight, fulfill the duties, look carefully" (Vines, 1978)," or be "watchful and exercise responsible care" (Webster, 1987), in fulfilling the charge and vision of feeding the flock of God." Henceforth, Apostle Peter asserts, take this vision, this oversight, and study and inspect it; become responsible for fulfilling this duty, vision and mission statement.

Filthy Lucre. Apostle Peter further proclaims, do not fulfil this vision for filthy lucre. Notice, it reads "filthy" lucre which describes a type of lucre. There is a distinction between lucre and "filthy" lucre. Lucre from the Latin word lucrum, means gain (Easton Bible Dictionary). Lucre is defined as mammon, money, revenue, earnings and funds. It is also defined as profit, riches and wealth. Lucre is used interchangeably with possessions, proceeds and resources (Webster, 1987).

Now, Apostle Peter did not say lucre; he specifically stated, "filthy lucre." In other words, do not feed the flock of God for "unclean lucre," "filthy" lucre. Filthy lucre is the opposite of lucre or "as it describes lucre in a negative connotation. Filthy lucre is underhand, vile and corrupt profits and bribes. Filthy lucre refers to unjust, covetousness and dishonest gain and profit. However, lucre in Greek is "aischrokerdes" which refers to filthy lucre or shamefully and greedy gain (Vines and Strong); it also means eager for base gain, (Strong's Greek Lexicon). "Kerdos" in Greek means gain an advantage or "betsa" (Hebrew) which means unjust gain and profit acquired by violence (Vines, 1970; Strong Hebrew Lexicon).

"Filthy" lucre is mentioned in both, Old and New Testament (Samuel 8:3; Titus 1: 7, 11; I Timothy 3:3,8 and I Peter 5:2). Samuel's sons, Joel and Abiah, turned after filthy lucre, bribes and perverted judgments, in the Old Testament. They did not walk in the ways of their father, Samuel. In essence, the sons committed extortion. In the New Testament, elders are commanded not to feed the flock of God for "filthy" lucre (I Peter 5:2). Bishops and deacons are commanded not to be greedy of "filthy" lucre (Titus 1:7; I Timothy 3:3, 8). Ministers are commanded not to teach for "filthy" lucre's sake (Titus 1:11).

How to Feed the Flock

Rather, Apostle Peter advocates, "feed the flock of God with a ready mind" (I Peter 5:2); a ready mind is an eager, prepared and willing mind. A mind that is ready to do the meat of God which is to feed the flock of God. Further, pastors are exhorted not to become lord over God's heritage, lineage, legacy, inheritance and bloodline (I Peter 5:3). The scripture reads,

> 5:3 "Neither as being lords over God's heritage, but being ensamples to the flock."

> 5:4 "And when the chief Shepherd shall appear, ye shall receive a crown that fadeth not away" (I Peter).

For Jesus is the "chief" Shepherd over the flock and pastors are the shepherds over the flock of the Church of God. Nonetheless, Jesus purposed pastors to become an example, ensample, and a model for the flock. In short, pastors are to lead by example. God has an even greater reward in mind for the bishops, pastors, elders and overseers than lucre. God plans, upon the chief Shepherd, Jesus, appearance, to reward this group of leaders, the powers that be, with a "crown of glory that fadeth not away (I Peter 5:2-4)

The Second Component of the Vision and Mission Statement

Overseer. Supportive of Apostle Peter's claim (I Peter 5:2) is Apostle Paul's claim (Acts 20:28). Apostle Paul's statement is the second component of the vision of the church of God; however, it includes a three-part component. Apostle Paul states in a similar passage of scripture, 20:28 "Take heed therefore unto yourselves, and to all the flock, which the Holy Ghost hath made you overseers, to feed the church of God, which he hath purchased with his own blood".

Apostle Paul is indeed advising pastors' of their pastoral duties of the church. Take heed unto yourself. The first duty of the second component which Apostle Paul mentions is overseer. Apostle Paul's charge to pastors is the call of overseer. However, what is often overlooked is the first words of advice in this passage, "take heed therefore unto yourselves." Now, Apostle Paul says, pastors, consider, recognize, regard, notice, listen and hearken, unto this: "The Holy Spirit made you overseers" of yourselves first and foremost, long before you pastored a church. Apostle Paul admonishes pastors to oversee themselves first (I Corinthian 6:9-20). Apostle Paul is advocating, maintain your body as a temple of the Holy Spirit (I Corinthian 6:19-20). Overseer your own body, spirit and soul. Strive to implement what you proclaim: abide in right standing and in good fellowship with the Lord.

Overseer all the flock. The second charge of the second component of the vision of the church of God is also concerning overseer. Apostle Paul is calling the pastors, elders and bishops to oversee all flock (Act 20:28). This command is given after the pastors have become overseer of themselves. Paul advises pastors to overseer, manage, inspect, examine and supervise all the flock, multitude and crowd. Further, leaders are to become eminent over, (natsach, Hebrew), and to care for, visit, judge and have oversight over, (paqad, Hebrew), all the flock. Apostle Paul advocates, leaders when you heed unto yourselves as the temple of the Holy Spirit, then can you oversee the flock so that each member will also maintain their bodies as the temple of the Holy Spirit (I Corinthians 6:9-20).

The Third Components of the Vision and Mission Statement

Feed the Church of God. The third charge of the second component of the vision of the church of God is concerning feeding the church of God. Apostle Paul's claim, "feed the church of God (Acts 20:28)," supports Apostle Peter's claim, "feed the flock of God" (I Peter 5:2). Apostle Paul advocates, pastors, bishops, elders and overseer "feed the church of God" which is the assembly (qahal [Hebrew]), congregation, true believers, mass, faith-believers) (Acts 20:28). Apostle Peter advises pastors to feed the flock of God which is the tsone (Hebrew, pomimnion (Greek), multitude and crowd.

In the New Testament, Jesus was cited in many scriptures, feeding the multitude and crowds. Jesus fed the multitude and crowd figuratively and literally. He fed the multitude the word by preaching and sharing the gospel. After Jesus preached to the multitude, on several occasions, Jesus fed them fish and barley loaves. Ensamples and examples that are cited in the Word that the Chief Shepherd, Jesus, performed, are the works that the Shepherd must perform.

Notice that these passage specifically distinguishes between the two groups of people, flock of God and the flock of the church of God. The pastor is to oversee over both groups of people under his care. Both Apostles, Peter and Paul, instruct the pastors to oversee all the flock of the congregation, both saints and the sinners alike. Further, they both instruct the pastors to feed God's flock which is both, the church of God and the flock in which the Holy Spirit made them overseer.

When feeding the "flock of God" or "the church of God," Apostles Paul and Peter advocate pastors, elders, bishops and overseers, feed the cattle. Metaphorically, tend to, feed and nourish the Christians by providing food through spiritual ministry. Foremost, feed the flock from the Word of God in a consistent and regular basis. Further, discipline and restore the flock of the church of God. Provide authority and assistance to the flock (Vines, 1979).

Apostle Paul speaks expressively about the church of

God. This church is not a building owned by man. Nor is it of a particular denomination or affiliation. The church that Apostle Paul speaks expressively about is "The Church of God." The church of God is a group of people that is composed of multitudes and crowds, the Greeks, the Barbarians, the Romans, the wise and the unwise" (Romans 1:14). It includes the civilized, the uncivilized, the learned, the unlearned, the scholars, the intelligent and the unintelligent. The Church of God is composed of sheep and shepherds. It is a group of churches, pastors, bishops, elders and overseers. It consists of Christ's followers (Saint Matthew 26:31; Saint Luke 2:8; and I Corinthians 9:7), Christ's disciples (Saint Luke 12:32), and is led by the chief Shepherd (I Peter 5:4).

The Church of God is owned by God and the flock of God is owned by God. In essence, God is declaring ownership of the Church (Acts 20:28) and ownership of the flock (I Peter 5:2). Apostle Paul declares that "God purchased the pastor, the flock (I Corinthians 6:19-20) and the church (Acts 20:28). Paul expounds the biblical truth that God has purchased the church with His own blood. Further, Paul states that the pastor and flock are included in the purchase and are a part of this church. The true essence and core of Christianity hinges on the biblical truth that God purchased the church and man with the blood of

Jesus (I Corinthians 6:20). For God so loved the world {sinners, flock, church}, that He gave his only begotten Son {as the item or person of exchange}, that whosoever believeth in Him should not perish, but have everlasting life (Saint John 3:16).

Apostle Paul speaks expressively about the Trinity of the Godhead and their role in the foundation of pastorship and church. All three had important roles in fulfilling the scripture. Apostle Paul explains the role of both the pastor and the church in this scripture. He states that: (1) The Father purchased and is therefore, the owners of the church of God, the flock of God, pastors, saints and sinners (Acts 20:28 and I Peter 5:2-4). (2) The Son is the price or exchange that was paid as He became the sacrificial Lamb that was slain at Calvary. It was the blood of the Lamb, the crucified life of Christ, that was the price for the church and the flock (Saint John 3:16). (3) The Holy Ghost made the pastor the overseer first, of his own body, and secondly, the body of the church (Acts 20:28).

27 Pastor, Shepherd and Overseer

The Powers that Be Jesus purposed pastors to oversee, prepare and feed the church. The pastors' role as overseer is one of management, supervision and administration of the church's business affairs. The pastor is also the executive and director of the church spiritual affairs. The foundation of the role of a pastor is sheer pastoring the flock, ministering to needs of the saved and unsaved, and providing Christian leadership. Further, authority and leadership are pillars of the pastorship and rightfully so. However, Apostle Paul said in many biblical translations,

> 13:1 "Let every soul be subject unto the higher powers. For there is no power but of God: the powers that be are ordained of God" (KJV).

> 13:1 "Let every man submit himself to the authorities of government. For all authority comes from God (CON): the authorities that now exist have been appointed by God" (MON).

Apostle Paul states, "For there is no authority except for God" (Romans 13:1, Darby). Therefore, the authority that the pastors have, "the powers that be," is delegated authority given to them by God and should be used in a humble way which further, builds the kingdom.

In my secular occupation as principal and administrator of an elementary school, authority is inherited in the position called positional power. As a principal, first and foremost, one is charge and has the authority to implement a vision for the school that is aligned with the vision of the District. One must share that vision and mission with all stakeholders of the school community. The vision should serve as the foundation that governs the activities within the school community.

Further, a principal has authority, positional power, to recommend to the superintendent qualified and certified employees for hiring, firing, termination and non-renewal. One has authority to execute corporal punishment, suspension, and expulsion of students enrolled in a school. Also, one has authority to direct, supervise and manage the affairs of the school which is in accordance to the school board policies and laws of the State of Mississippi. However, the positional power and authority inherited in an elementary school principal are grounded in the laws of education.

In the spiritual calling of the pastor as an overseer of a church, authority is inherited in the position called positional power. As a pastor, first and foremost, one is charge with and has the authority to implement a vision for the church that is aligned with the vision that God has for the church. The vision must be shared with the members of the church. The vision should be the key factor that governs the activities of the church and that will usher in the kingdom to come.

Further, the pastor has authority, positional power, to recommend to the Board of Trustees spiritually and naturally, qualified and certified Christian employees who will unite to fulfil the vision and mission of not only their church, but also "the church of God." The pastor has authority to direct, supervise and manage the affairs of the church so that the vision will be realized. However, the positional power and authority inherited in a pastor are grounded in the guidelines within the Bible and the power granted from God.

An elementary school principal also operates from delegated power. The delegated power and authority are grounded in the Local and State Superintendent and the members of both the Local and State Board of Education. All authority is given by the Laws of the State of Mississippi Educational System. The principal therefore, operates within the Laws of the State of Mississippi Educational System.

A pastor of a church also operates from delegated power. The delegated power and authority in which a pastor operates, "the powers that be,' are ordained of God" (Roman 13:1). In most churches, the Board of Trustees operates the affairs of the church. Yes, their assistance is needed in some areas, i.e., the physical maintenance and other decision-making activities. However, according to the Order of God and the Bible, the Board of Trustees was not given delegated authority to implement the vision of the church. The Board of Trustees is to be subject to the higher powers, to God, primarily and to the pastor, secondarily. For "the powers that be,' are ordained of God." Apostle Paul says in Roman,

> 13:1 "Let every soul be subject unto the higher powers. For there is no power but of God: the powers that be are ordained of God" (KJV).

> 13:1 "Let every man submit himself to the authorities of government. For all authority comes from God (CON): the authorities that now exist have been appointed by God" (MON).

Lastly, as a principal, one has personal power that is inherited in one's personality. This power is called charisma or presence. Charisma is the ability to get the job done through influence. This personal power is often the root of politics in the church. However, this power is desired but is not necessary. The dual powers, positional and personal, working hand-in-hand with delegated power are great to move a school to the attainment of set goals.

The pastor, shepherd or overseer of a church, the powers that be, also has personal power that is inherited in one personality. Keeping it spiritual, I call this power the Anointing, the Gift(s) or the Holy Ghost. The Anointing is the ability to get the job done through favor and the through the supernatural realm. However, this power is necessary and desired to accomplish spiritual tasks in earthly situations. The dual powers of positional and the Anointing, working hand-in-hand with the delegated authority are necessary to move a church toward the attainment of the set vision given by God for "the church of God."

Vision For The Pastor

In a very familiar passage of scripture, Apostle Paul speaks expressively to Timothy concerning pastors and the vision for the pastors' house. One will find throughout the Bible that God the Father charts the path and Jesus the Son models the way for Christians to follow. In essence, Jehovah Adonai leads and teaches by examples and ensamples through the Word, Jesus that became flesh.

Timothy believes that a pastor should rule his own house and rule it well (Timothy 3:4). This belief has powerful implications for the Pastor. The ability to "rule his house and rule it well" is symbolic of many concepts in the scripture. Firstly, this statement is symbolic of power and authority in a headship or leadership role. (A) This implies that a Pastor should be given the power and authority by the congregation that is already inherited in the position, to execute the leadership role of the organization. (B) This further implies that a Pastor should be able to lead, supervise, administrate and orchestrate the successful activities of the church. (C) The Pastor should be allowed to share and implement his inspired vision for the organization.

Secondly, the ability to "rule his house and rule it well" is symbolic of management of his/her own physical body. Apostle Paul stated that the "body is the temple of the Holy Spirit (I Corinthian 6:18). (A) This implies that the Pastor should manage and maintain balance in his own body. (B) His/her body should be spiritually in tuned to the Holy Spirit, mentally alert and prepared with the Word of God, physically strong to endure the warfare inherited in this position, socially aware of the needs of the church and psychological nourished to sustained humility and abstained from narcissism. (C) This further implies that a Pastor should prosper and be in good health, even as his/her soul prosper (3 John 1:2). (D) A pastor's feet should be shod with preparation. (E) A pastor should study to show himself approved unto God, one who can rightly divide the Word of truth to his/her appointed church.

Thirdly, the scripture states that the husband is the

head of the wife and must therefore love his wife as Christ loves the church; a husband is commanded to love his wife as he loves himself (Ephesians 5:23;25;28). Think for a second, if a man doesn't know how to rule his own house, can he rule over the church of God (Timothy 3:5)? Women must learn to submit so this order can be accomplished.

The ability to rule one's house, provides a pastor with certified and simulation rehearsals and experiences to rule the church. When a pastor rules his house well, he acquires first hand experiences that becomes a repertoire of information that may be utilized in performing the business and functions of the church. For instance, the home encompasses one family that has a smaller number of persons, personalities and needs and the church encompasses many families, each having a number of persons with a vast range of personalities and needs. When a pastor rules the small number of persons, personalities and needs well, he is ready for the promotion that encompasses a large families, personalities and needs.

However, each ministry, ruling of the home and church, is equally important and is ordained by God. Each ministry deals with leading people to Jesus and feeding people the bread of life. Therefore, pastors must pray for spiritual consciousness and intuition to rule and oversee effectively. He who rules, should strive to rule well.

Pastor and First Lady

The responsibilities of a pastor and spouse as overseers of the church are tremendous. They live in the limelight being informally observed and evaluated by mankind. Although, God judges the heart, the inner man, the church community does not follow the same pattern. The church community inspects the pastor and spouse for every duty and responsibility that are inherited in the positions of pastor, first lady, husband, wife, father, mother, Christian and human. They are inspected from both spiritual and secular views and by both spiritual and secular communities. If one or both have a secular occupation, the fire gets hotter and the yardstick criteria gets tougher. The scope and sequence of the personal evaluations are escalated. These dual roles may fuel the fire and may oftentimes, diminish the effectiveness of their leadership. However, there are numerous accounts where the pastors' effectiveness is enhanced because of fulfilling dual responsibilities in both the secular and spiritual communities.

Notice, I said at the beginning of the last paragraph, the responsibilities of a "pastor and spouse." If indeed the pastor is married, this headship, leadership of the church, should typifies the example of Jesus and the Church. Remember, and the two becomes one and should be inseparable by man and/or the church. Furthermore, most scriptures that allude or share knowledge concerning husband and wife, speak about the example relationship of Jesus and the church.

Often times, one wants to separate the husband and wife when it comes to fulfilling the duties and the responsibilities of the church. When a Congregation, the deacons or the trustees hires a pastor, this Board expects the pastor to pastor the church and the wife or spouse of the pastor to take a submissive role and wear a hat with matching shoes and purse or to wear an outfit that matches that of the pastor . The two, pastor and spouse, vowed long before the congregation stepped in the scene, to a life of oneness. They further vowed that only death could depart them from each other. The spouse of the pastor becomes pastor by the inherited duties of the marriage and by positional duties, i.e., President of the United States' spouse becomes president by the inherited duties of the marriage and by positional power and duties. The Congregation nor the Board cannot and should not try to separate the two. Again only death, which is an enemy to man, can and should separate a pastor and spouse or a husband and wife.

A pastor and spouse must be prepared for the momentum responsibility of overseers of the church, a body of believers, as they fulfilled the roles of husband and wife to each other. While fulfilling these dual roles of both pastors, wife, husband and overseer, a marriage may encountered many, some unnecessary, trials and hardships in undertaking this tremendous calling and election. People may become cruel toward the pastor's relationship with the spouse and/or with their family because of a selfish agenda and an unspiritual motivation.

28 The First Lady

The position of First Lady is more spiritually fulfilling than the title. Oftentimes one is caught up in the title and neglect the inherited duties. The Pastor's wife is and will be a helpmeet in roles and positions. It is ordained for wife to be a helpmeet. The pastor should allow her to perform her duties. However, she must be spiritually and physically equipped and prepared for the role.

I pray that the pastor's wife doesn't become snared by the glamour and glory of the position of the first lady! It is most advantageous spiritually for the first lady to focus on the works of this position and ministry. I encourage the pastor's wife to work while it's day; night shall come when no one will work (St. John 9:4). I encourage the first lady to work with the measure of faith that she has and to work for the glory of God. I pray that all first ladies, pastor's wives, follow the example and duplicate the services of the real First Lady.

The real First Lady, the church, Jesus' bride is being purged this very moment so that she can receive her Groom, the High Priest. The real First Lady stands open every Sunday, hopefully every day, to minister to the needs of the wounded, the broken-hearted, the captives, and souls who need deliverance.

The real First Lady is actually the Last Lady who is prophesied to come on the scene after her preparatory stage is completed! The real first Lady is the Church who is the last one to wed. And "the last shall be first."

First Lady, please experience a glimpse of the glory of the Lord. Experience walking in the cool of the Garden as Eve did. Eve imitated and replicated no one. She knew her role and performed it well for the most part until she was enticed and beguiled by the serpent. Know that you are in a key position to help win souls to Christ. Fulfil your mission with all diligence.

First Lady, I know and share the struggle in fulfilling this awesome and sacred role as pastor's wife. Your role is a difficulty one; it's a cross to bear. However, adopt the mission and role of the First Lady, the church. Be prepared and available to minister to the needs of the wounded and broken-hearted. Be prepared to be a help-meet to your groom, your husband, with his awesome responsibility in preparing the Church, bride, for the Jesus' Kingdom. Be prepared to be a help meet to the groom, the Lord Jesus Christ, in preparing the earth for the coming of His Kingdom.

First Ladies, I encourage each of you to become the first lady to bear witness of the coming of Our Savior. Become the first lady to feed the poor, clothe the naked, and visit the sick. Commitment to a life, an election and the call of helpmeet as a pastor's wife. Be sure of your call and election (I Corinthians 7:20-24; II Peter 1:10) as helpmeet. Truly, many are called and chosen to be a pastor's wife but few are elected, prepared for and committed to the service of a pastor's wife.

Remember, the position of First Lady is not the way to everlasting life and happiness; Jesus is the Way to enter into a life of happiness and contentment. The visible role of a first lady is not actual the truth of the whole matter, the other half should be told. The other half must be proclaimed in the highways, byways and uttermost parts of the world. The other half that hath not being told is: the church is the First Lady who is the bride of Jesus Christ, Our Savior.

Pastors' wife, you married your husband; you are his helpmeet. Help meet your husband's responsibilities as an overseer of the church. Become a Delilah and provide a lap for your husband's head; become a Ruth and show forth loyalty to your Boaz. Your Boaz came as First Lady Deborah Morton proclaimed. Serve your king with reverence until the coming of the King.

Pastors' wife, perform the weaker vessel's duties and obligations as you assist your husband in the ministry. Minister to your husband with eucalyptus and candle light baths or whatever. Minister to your husband by providing your husband with his favorite herbal teas or drink that only you know.

Make a quality decision today to develop a relationship with Jesus Christ. The same Spirit that your husband worships is the same Spirit you must worship. You truly become a fulfilled being when you worship God in spirit and in truth. Woman, thou art truly loosed as Bishop T. D. Jakes proclaimed, in liberty to worship God in truth and in the beauty of holiness.

Wife, you are not required to worship your husband or his ministry; God is a jealous God! You are required to obey, honor and reverence your husband.

I thank God that I breathe my Adonai, for it was God who blew life back into me; I feast on God, as I meditate on His Word day and night. I live God, as I dwell in the house of God inquiring about His secrets and mysteries.

29 Weaker Vessel

As the weaker vessel, a pastor's wife is called to fulfil a role of "Sanctification." However, if one views the calling and election in the same regard as Christ does, one would be careful to exemplify the traits that Jesus expects from his bride, the church. Jesus sees the role as a call to sanctification and spiritual oneness with Him. The traits and conditions that Jesus expects are ones of purity, chastity, holiness. For Jesus will return for his bride the church that has met certain criteria. The criteria are spotlessness, flawlessness, wrinkle-free, and blemish-free. This role of sanctification for the weaker vessel and pastor's wife is one that sets one aside for the sole purpose of assisting in the preparation for the kingdom that is to come.

The weaker vessel and pastor's wife are ministries. The wife is also called to the ministry of helps (I Corinthians). For the wife is a helpmeet exclusively to her husband first and foremost. The weaker vessel is to meet the needs of her husband in the home with reverence and honor. When success is achieved in meeting the needs in the home as the scripture suggests, the weaker vessel is equipped with the success to assist her husband in meeting the needs of the church. God has an order and his order is for the weaker vessel to show forth love and kindness first in the home.

Perfect practice at home on how to show forth love and kindness to others is a tremendous help in showing the same to the church and community. In I Corinthians 13, Charity does begin in the home and spreads and permeates aboard.

The working of love and all of God's laws and precepts are first for the home and then for others. Oftentimes, we as humans want to show to the world what we have not practice and displayed in the home. However, home is where you get your practice; home is where you perfect the fulfilling of God's word. When one experiences perfect practice in the home, then one can have successful experiences with others, particularly the church.

The role as weaker vessel is so duplex that God outlined explicit and precise details for one to accomplish this task. The weaker vessel is to love, obey and reverence her husband. This role was so complex that the scripture admonished the older women to teach the younger women how to love their husband (Titus 2:4).

When answering the call as pastor's wife, your first priority is to assist your husband in the fulfilling of his needs at home first and then in the church. If one see the calling in the light that Christ had in mind or will, it a role many women will not chose. Oftentimes, it a role that chooses you.

Oftentimes, the calling and election of a wife and pastor's wife is often misinterpreted and fulfilled from the natural perspective of glamour and prestige, however, it is quite the contrary. The weaker vessel and the pastor's wife are a call to: (1) And election that God ordains; (2) Sanctification; (3) Minister to your, husband, home and church and in that order; and, (4) Love as Jesus love and gave his life for all.

For those women who are ministers, evangelists, or a pastor of a church, you still are the weaker vessel if you are married. As you fulfill you role as pastor, you wear big shoes. As you reverence and obey "The Lord," you must also reverence and obey "the lord," your husband.

30 Church, The Great Mystery

Jesus Christ is the chief executive and director of the church's spiritual affairs. Christ is the head of the church and the savior of the body (Ephesians 5:23). The God of our Lord Jesus Christ placed all matters under the feet of Christ and gave Him the headship over all things concerning the church, which is his body (Ephesians 5:22;23). Paul concludes the matter when he said, "Jesus is the head of the body, the church" (Colossians 1:18).

Let's look spiritually into this concept: The church belongs to God who purchased it with Jesus' blood. This concept points to many truths and is a mystery. First, God gave his Son, Jesus as a sacrificial Lamb on the cross for the sins of the people of the world, the church. God so loved the world, that He gave His only begotten Son, the price, (Saint John 3:16) as a ransom for mankind to be saved.

> 3:16   "For God so loved the world, that He gave his only begotten son that whosoever believe in Him should not perish: but should have everlasting life" (Saint John).

Secondly, Paul state in I Corinthians that "your body is the temple (church) of the Holy Ghost which is in you, which ye have of God, and ye are not your own. Your body is the church (temple) where the Holy Spirit (Godhead: God, Jesus, Holy Spirit) abides. This body, church, temple, was purchased by God. God owns and abides in your body. Your body is the church (I Corinthians 6:19). The church is owned by God. The church is Christ's body (Ephesians 5:23). "Jesus is the head of the body, the church" (Colossians 1:18).

> 18 What? Know ye not that your body is the temple of the Holy Ghost which is in you, which ye have of God, and ye are not your own?
>
> 19 For ye are bought with a price: therefore glorify God in your body, and in your spirit, which are God's (I Corinthians 6).

31 Church -The Body of Christ

I pray for the church, the members of the congregation, who feel that God bestowed upon them the responsibility of oversee the pastor's marriage. I weep for the church that judges their pastor's marriage to the point that the judgment is one that puts asunder what God has put together.

Pastor, is it difficult to separate yourself from the duties and functions of the church and easy to separate yourself from the duties and functions of the home? Is it difficult to separate from the church family and easy to separate from your family? Should there be division among you? Should there be division among the church? Should there be division in a home? Do you know that a house divided will not stand? In the going forth of your ministry, the family is first, at all times and in all things? Pastor, there should not be division among you. Pastors, should you depart from your wife physically, soulically or spiritually (I Corinthians 7:15b) for church work? Entreat your wife not to leave you or return from following you physically, soulically or spiritually (Ruth 1:16)

I weep for the church that records and judges their pastor's marriage to the extent that it forces the pastor to treat his wife the way God doesn't instructed. Isn't this a sure sign that something or someone is out of line with the precepts and laws of Jehovah Adonai? Pastors, is it easy to treat the church with the utmost respect and highest regard and treat your home differently? Pastors, is it is easy to treat the church, which is in the public's eye and is judged by many with the utmost respect and highest regard and treat the home, which is private and judge by few differently? Do you remember, what is done privately will soon manifest? Pastors, should you depart from your wife physically, soulically or spiritually (I Corinthians 7:15b). Entreat your wife not to leave you or depart from following you physically, soulically or spiritually (Ruth 1:16). Return to your first love.

I weep for the church that ostracizes, demeans and curses the pastor and/or the first lady. Isn't this behavior typical? Isn't this behavior being replicated? Was it not the church that play an intrigued role in Jesus' crucifixion? Does the congregation realize that what you do to the wife, you do unto the husband? Are they not one flesh? Isn't the church in a preparatory stage for the coming of her Groom? Is the church mature enough to judge Jesus' ordained and anointed ones? Is the church charged with the responsibility of judging Jesus' ordained and anointed one? Are the saints charged with the responsibility of judging the world? Or are the saints charged with the responsibility of judging the church? Should the church be prepare itself to be judged? Selah.

Church and members, why do you put asunder what God has put together? Why not seek to do your own business? Let this business be the business of the Lord. Become steadfast and unmovable during the preparatory period. Let God complete His perfect work in you so that you may be completely ready and prepared when his Kingdom comes.

Two Wives

A true soul mate must know how to forsake all others as he unites with his wife to form the oneness that Christ so often makes reference. The "others" that must be placed in priority might be that church that the pastor shepherds. Think for a second! If a pastor treats the church as if it is his wife, then who is chosen to become Jesus' bride? Then who will Jesus return to marry? Remember, there is going to be a wedding. Jesus is going to be the groom and the church is going to be the bride.

32 Pastor's Family - The First Family

I pray for the pastor's family, especially the children, who are caught up in a life of ministry and of giving and sharing of their father. I often wonder, what is their thought process? Would they rate the life of pastor's children as a life that is being trained up or strained up in way of righteousness? Do they know their true place in their father's heart? Do they know their role in the church family? Do they feel secondary to the children of the church? Are they so proud of Daddy that they can wait patiently in line for his attention, love and affection?

Fathers, be careful not to provoke your children to wrath. Be careful that there are no later regrets. Carpe Diem! Seize the opportunities while your babies are little to provide them with quality time that can't be substitute by others.

As a child development specialist and consultant, I would encourage you to schedule a block of time with your children to nourish them in the admonition of the Lord. Place such value on this scheduled time that an interruption would be classified as disrespectful conduct. Build such a solid foundation with your little girl that when she becomes a teenager she wouldn't need the other to fulfil what Daddy didn't give. Build such a firm foundation with your son that love and blessing flow from his lips. Commit to your child's upbringing. Commit to the germination of your seeds so that they grow up to be seeds of righteousness.

In the movie "Preacher's Wife", the son, Justin Edmund, echoed thoughts about his parents as he sat on the pew during worship services. My daughter Grace often verbalizes how perplexed she becomes at the contrasting behaviors that are displayed at home and in the church. I wonder if Grace's thoughts are like the thoughts of the son in the movie. As my daughter sat in the choir stand listening to her father deliver his message and as she canvases the congregation, I would give a cup of herbal tea or whatever to read the tablets of her soul and to hear her thoughts and feel what her heart feels. Pastors' children really know the inside story. And they do have a story. I sense in my spirit that we will hear from the pastor's children very soon.

In reference to the movie, "Preacher's Wife," the mission that was to be accomplished by the pastor, first lady, and the church was very simple and the process appeared to present a grand ole time. Is the main objective of our existence really simple and we make it complicated? However, in the movie, the needs of the wife were secondary to the needs of the church family. There was very little to no interaction between the son and his father. I pray that this scenario is atypical of the pastor's relationship with his family and the church. Sadly to admit, I believe it depicts a real life situation.

The responsibilities of a pastor's wife and children, are awesome just as the responsibilities of being a pastor. Most families are not prepared for this responsibility nor could the members of the family survive such trials and hardship that must be encountered when undertaking this tremendous calling. Pastors, I echo the advice that Paul gives in Ephesians 6:4, provoke not your children to wrath and raise them up in the admonition of the Lord.

Please understand, I am the messenger to spread this message abroad. I am only the vessel that holds the pen or rather punches the keys. I am only the mouth piece. Jesus is the Author. However, I do believe that each Pastor's sentiment is: As for me and my house, we will worship and serve the Lord. HALLELUJAH!

PART EIGHT
33 I Thirst
... If any man thirst, let him come unto me and drink. Saint John 7:37

My Tree searched day and night reading spiritually related and inspirational literature, e.g., the many different biblical translations and the many biblical commentaries and help guides for answers. He thirst vehemently and urgently for knowledge and truth. He wanted so desperately to share revelation knowledge and impart a rhema word to his flock. It appeared that if he only could have remembered that Proverbs 1:7 declared that the fear of God is the beginning of knowledge, then he would at least had a true starting point and a solid foundation for quenching thirst. Further, if he also could have remembered and meditated on the following passage, he would have known that an intimate relationship is the route to quenching one's thirst. The passage stated,

"In the last days, that great day of the feast, Jesus stood and cried, saying, If any man thirst, let him come unto me and drink. He that believeth on me, as the scripture hath said, out of his belly shall flow rivers of living water" (Saint John 7:37-38).

The implication of the verses is deeply imbedded in one receiving and accepting the Holy Spirit into their life and operating in the fruits and gifts of the Holy Spirit. It implies that when a lingering thirst occurs in one's life, there is a craving and passion for a spiritual and intimate relationship with the complete Godhead, God the Father, Jesus the Son and the Holy Spirit the Comforter. This passage offers an invitation, provides guidance, as well as the pathway for one's thirst to be quenched. A channel has also been strategically laid out in this passage for direct connection to and communication with Jesus by way of the Holy Spirit for one's thirst not only to be quenched temporarily but eternally. The only criteria outlined in this passage in order for man to receive this everlasting flow of rivers of living waters, according to Jesus is to: (1) Come, which is an invitation; (2) Drink, which is a partaking, and; (3) Believe, which is an act of faith. Moreover, an invitation is given to all men in Revelation 22:17.

> "And the Spirit and the bride say, Come. And let him that heareth say, Come. And let him that is athirst come. And whosoever will, let him take the water of life freely."

If my tree could have grasped and accepted this concept which includes the invitation, the partaking and the believing, then he would have been connected with and directed to the pathway that led to the Source who could have quenched his thirst with an everlasting flow of rivers of living waters (Saint John 7:37-38). Whether his thirst was quenched with the knowledge and truth he sought, I will never know. I do know that Jesus is the genuine source of truth. For Jesus is the way, the truth and the life (Saint John 14:6). The way to the truth is through Jesus. Therefore, in order to know the truth, one must know Jesus. Furthermore, Jesus, "the spirit of truth will guide one to all truth" (Saint John 16:13b).

First Lady Eve, in the Garden of Eden, was also thirsty for knowledge. Eve was so avidly thirsty for knowledge, truth and wisdom that she became vulnerable and eager to drink any knowledge that she felt would quench her thirst. First Lady Eve had already received the unadulterated truth and knowledge given to her directly from the True and Living God; therefore, her thirst should have been quenched, she should have been satisfied and she should have experienced a cup that overflowed. First Lady Eve received knowledge directly from the Source where all truth abides and originates. Eve experienced and beheld the evidences of substance that we as Christians only have hope of experiencing and beholding. First Lady Eve, along with Adam, walked in the cool of the evening with the True One and; therefore, received knowledge on a daily basis. What more can a person, a saint, desire than to be in the presence of Almighty?

The question was posed, "What more can a person, namely, First Lady Eve, desire than to be in the presence of the Source of all Truth?" First Lady Eve desired and thirsted for more than the daily communion she received from the Lord. Eve desired and thirsted for a greater dispersion of knowledge. However, the serpent to whom First Lady Eve communicated her desires and thirst, also had a desire and thirst. The serpent thirsted to commune with First Lady Eve in the same manner in which God communed with both Adam and Eve in the garden. The serpent desired and implemented a surreptitious plan to become the Lord of the Heaven; as a result of this rebellious act, Lucifer was thrown out of heaven and was found in the Garden of Eden fulfilling his thirst with First Lady Eve.

The serpent desired and thirsted to become the "God" as God the Father. Lucifer, thereby, anticipated the clandestine possession of all power and all knowledge. The serpent willed and attempted to duplicate any acts or services performed by God that in turn would render him, (the serpent), as omnipotent as God the Father. The very act or service that the serpent simulated and rendered unto First Lady Eve was the impartation of knowledge. This knowledge was unlike the knowledge that God imparted into First Lady Eve and First Man Adam. The serpent imparted fictitious knowledge into First Lady Eve's untainted and pure belief system that rendered her impotent and imperfect. First Lady Eve yield to the serpent's perception of reality. Eve succumbed to the voice of the serpent as the serpent communicated to her concerning knowledge of godship, good and evil. First Lady Eve believed that she would become a "god" like the Lord our God is and could thereby, discern between good and evil (Genesis 3:5).

In the true essences of the word "god", Eve and Adam were fulfilling that role in the garden. Adam and First Lady Eve were not the Supreme Creator of the world; but, they were Supreme Being over the Garden of Eden. Adam and First Lady Eve were the "god" or pastor of the Garden of Eden; hence, all living creatures in the Garden of Eden were subdued by them as they were given dominion over every living creature. However, First Lady Eve never became the "God" that the serpent led her to believe she would become. She did not become a "God" like Jehovah Adonai is nor did Lucifer become a "God" when he thirst for authority in heaven. Thus, both Lady Eve and Lucifer were denied entrance back into their dwellings, Garden of Eden and Heaven. First Lady Eve was put out of the Garden of Eden and Lucifer was thrown out of Heaven which was the penalty for insubordination and disobedience.

Eve and Adam became cognizant of the principle of "good and evil" from that day forth as they paid a great penalty for eating from the forbidden tree. This entire ordeal came about primarily because of Eve's thirst for knowledge and truth and Eve's submission of will to the serpent for betrayal and deception to occur. Consequently, we all suffered because of First Lady Eve's choice.

There are many questions that can be asked as a result of Eve's action in the Garden of Eden. Why didn't First Lady Eve utilize the knowledge that God had initially given her? Was not Eve satisfied with the knowledge God imparted into her daily? Did First Lady Eve doubt that God had given her the truth? Did Eve believe that God had not given her the whole truth? Did not Eve believe that God had withheld a portion of the truth from her? Couldn't Eve choose to do that which was good and opposed that which was evil? Why didn't First Lady Eve realize that choosing to do "good" meant obedience to God and to his commandment? Could not Eve discern that choosing to do "evil" or being contrary to God's instructions, meant disobedience to God and to his commandment? Why did Eve realize that choosing "good" meant eating only from the tree that God had commanded? Selah.

We are all created to operate as free will and moral beings. We are created with a will and the ability to choose. Although, God has put in us an inherent ability to know what is good and what is evil, we seem to struggle with the appropriately and spiritually correct choices to resolve the many dilemmas we face. God has created us so much in His likeness until we simply know what is a good or/and evil choice even if we had not studied or/and experienced that particular topic or issue. God is the kind of Creator who created His creations with "intuitive spirits", knowing the difference in good and evil.

34 The Crucifixion - Mission Accomplished
After this, Jesus knowing that all things were now accomplished, that the scripture might be fulfilled, saith, I thirst. Saint John 19:28

Let's examine two occasions in the bible when Jesus implied or declared that he thirsted. At the crucifixion, the point that Jesus knew His mission was accomplished, He declared, "I thirst."   The specific passage in Saint John 19:28 states that "after this, Jesus knowing that all things were now accomplished, that the scripture might be fulfilled, saith, I thirst." Was this thirst a physical thirst, that followed many excruciating hours of physical torture, internal struggles and spiritual battles (Saint Matthew 27:27-31; Saint Mark 15:17-20, and; Saint Luke 23:34-38)?

I believe that because Jesus was scourged during the preparation for his crucifixion, Jesus was thirsty. Jesus experienced a sensation of dryness in his mouth and throat that was associated with a desire for liquids or a need for a drink (Webster New Collegiate Dictionary). However, Jesus was so committed to fulfilling the will of God the Father that He realized his physical need after the work of God was accomplished. Jesus willingly fulfilled His ultimate mission that God had given him for man's redemption. Then, Jesus declared, mission accomplished and proceeded to attend to his thirst, a higher order of need, according to Abraham

Maslow's Hierarchy of Needs.

The soldiers of the governor heard Jesus utterance of his thirst. In a mockery manner, the soldiers proceeded to give Jesus something to quench his thirst. Psalms 69:21b declared, "And in my thirst they gave me vinegar to drink." The soldiers attempted to satisfy Jesus' thirst by giving him vinegar mixed with water. The scripture stated:

> "Now there was set a vessel full of vinegar: and they filled a sponge with vinegar and put it upon hyssop and put it to his mouth" (Saint John 19:29).

This was not an acceptable drink for Jesus' thirst as he stood nailed and maimed on the cross at Golgotha (Hebrew) or Calvary (Saint Luke 23:33). Or was it? In Matthew 27:34, Jesus would not drink the vinegar mingled with gall or water. Jesus refused the drink; although, he was thirsty. In Saint Luke 15:23, "they gave him to drink wine mingled with myrrh: but he received it not." Jesus had gone through such an ordeal that it seemed that any liquids would have satisfied his thirst. However, when Jesus tasted the drink, "he would not drink" it.

Jesus refused the drink that the soldiers gave him. Many questions flood my mind as I ponder over Jesus' action. Why did Jesus say, "I thirst?" Why would Jesus refuse a drink when he was thirsty? Did he not ask for a drink? When Jesus stated, "I thirst," what did he mean? Was he not thirst for a drink? Any drink? Why did Jesus thirst? Was this thirst figuratively or literally? Was Jesus thirsty to do the will of His Father? Was Jesus thirsty to return back to His Father? Was Jesus thirsty to give man a second chance for redemption? Was Jesus thirsty to demonstrate God's love for the world? Was Jesus thirsty to demonstrate to the world that God had made a provision for man to have eternal life? Was Jesus' thirst fulfilled? Is the power of choice a factor in this scenario? Is the power of will a factor in this scenario? Selah.

PART NINE

35 The Samaritan Woman
. . . Give me to drink. Saint John 4:7

Let's examine the second account in the bible when Jesus implied that he thirsted (Saint John 4:2-42). After Jesus had departed from Judea and before he entered into Galilee, he traveled through Samaria. In Samaria, Jesus stopped at and sat on Jacob's well after a long journey. Jesus had traveled to the point that he was exhausted. Jesus was physically tired and wearied from this journey; therefore, he stopped to supposedly revive himself by getting a drink from Jacob's well early in the day, at the sixth hour (Saint John 4:6). Jesus had sat at the well a while when, along came a Samaritan woman to the well to draw water. The scripture stated that Jesus said unto the Samaritan woman, "Give me to drink" (Saint John 4:7).

Come now, let us reason together. Why did Jesus initiate a conversation with the Samaritan woman? Why was the Samaritan woman drawing water so early in the day? Was the Samaritan woman an outcast? Did she draw water at the sixth hour because she was a Samaritan and a woman? Did she draw water early in the day to avoid trouble? Why did the disciples leave Jesus alone at the well? Where were the disciples? For what was Jesus thirsty?

What type thirst was this? What could possible quench Jesus' thirst? Was this a symbolic thirst? Was this an ironic request? Selah.

When one travels as Jesus does, it is customary to at least take a dish or utensil to draw drinking water from a well. It appeared that Jesus' armor bearer or one of his disciples would have made provision for Jesus' need in this capacity before "going into the city to buy meat" (Saint John 4:8). Further, Eastern travelers frequently carry and utilize a leather bucket to draw water from public wells (Dakes, 1992). However, it was not mentioned whether Jesus traveled with such gears; but in the Samaritan woman's observation of Jesus, she stated that Jesus did not have anything to draw water.

The Samaritan woman was very inquisitive as she asked Jesus many significant questions. The Samaritan woman was not eager to obliged Jesus because he was a Jew. She desired more intense dialogue from Jesus; however, she realized the racial barriers that existed between the Jews and the Samaritans. The Samaritans woman asked Jesus, "how could a Jew ask a Samaritan woman for a drink when the Jews had no dealing with the Samaritans?" She needed answers to many questions that were common to their racial and her personal dilemma. Because of the nature of the questions asked, did the

Samaritan woman have a thirst that needed quenching? Did she have a void that needed fulfilling? I believe that the Samaritan woman thirst had not been quenched. I also believe that the Samaritan woman knew that only Jesus himself could quench her thirst. I believe that the Samaritan woman's void had not been fulfilled. For she had five husbands; yet, her thirst was not quenched or her void was not fulfilled, not even with the sixth man who was not her husband (Saint John 4:18). But with Jesus giving her a drink of living water, I believe that thirst was quenched.

The dialogue between Jesus and the Samaritan woman continued. Jesus answered the Samaritan woman's question and said, "If you know the gift of God, and who it is who asked, 'give me to drink', you would ask me, and I would give you living water." Jesus was such a great conversationalist; for he did not boldly and arrogantly proclaim, I can give you the gift of God because I am a prophet. But he confidently and gently stated his response in such an awesome manner until the Samaritan woman desired additional information concerning the gift of God and who Jesus was.

As the conversation intensified, it was obvious that the Samaritan woman was not cognizant of the gift of God nor of Jesus' identification and/or credentials. Jesus made this apparent when he stated, "If you know the gift of God and if you know who it is who asked for a drink." However, the response from Jesus ignited in the Samaritan woman two issues that could possibly quench her thirst and fulfilled her void. These two issues that sprung forth from Jesus' reply were: (1) The gift of God, and; (2) The living water.

Intuitively and psychologically, the Samaritan woman knew that Jesus was fulfilling her needs as they talked. She prolonged the conversation by asking Jesus a second question. The Samaritan woman said unto Jesus "Sir, thou hast nothing to draw with, and the well is deep: from whence then hast thou that living water?' 'Art thou greater than our father Jacob, who gave us the well, and drank thereof himself, and his children, and his cattle" (Saint John 4:11-12)?

The Samaritan woman was very curious when asking the second question. She first proceeded to attended to Jesus' request for a drink; then, she inquired about the living water. The Samaritan was so curious that she wanted to know about Jesus accomplishments and his greatness. In essence, she ask Jesus, so, what can you do for me or what have you done for others. The Samaritan woman thought, we know Jacob our father and we know what Jacob has done for us. She stated, Jacob was such a great man; he gave us this well. Not only did Jacob give us this well, but Jacob, his children and his cattle drank from this well.

The Samaritan woman implied, what have you done? Who are you? Are you a Prophet? In essence she asked Jesus, "What can you do for me or what have you done for others."

In reply to the Samaritan woman's question, "from whence then hast thou that living water," Jesus answered and said unto her, "Whosoever drink of this water shall thirst again. But whosoever drink of the water that I shall give him shall never thirst but, the water that I shall give him shall be in him a well of water springing up to everlasting life" (Saint John 4:13-14).

At this juncture in the conversation, Jesus offered to the Samaritan woman the gift of God and the living water. The Samaritan woman desperately and genuinely wanted this living water as she eagerly stated her reasons for wanting the water. The woman saith unto Jesus, "Sir give me this water, that: (1) I thirst not; neither, (2) Come hither to draw" (Saint John 4:15). I believe at this point in the conversation, the Samaritan woman knew that Jesus was least concerned about quenching his physical and temporary thirst and more concerned about quenching her spiritual thirst.

The Samaritan woman had a genuine desired to quench her thirst and to fill the void that lingered even after five husbands and a sixth man. The Samaritan woman wanted this water to quench her thirst. She knew that if Jesus quenched her thirst with the living water, that this water would also fill her void. She knew that if her void was filled that she would not have to "come hither to draw" from the well or to meet a seventh man; for the six men she had did not quench her thirst or fill her void. Only the man from Galilee could and did quench her thirst and fill her void.

There are many questions that I ponder in this situation. What occurred in the time frame when Jesus was alone at Jacob's well before the Samaritan woman arrived? Was Jesus in dire need of a drink? Was Jesus in dire need of a drink from Jacob's well? Did Jesus have ample time to draw water before the Samaritan woman approached Jacob's well? Did he have a dish in which to draw from the well? What was the objective of the question Jesus asked, "Give me to drink?" Was the question Jesus asked the Samaritan woman an icebreaker? Was the conversation between Jesus and the Samaritan woman an initiative to break down the racial barriers that stood between the Jews and the Samaritans? Did Jesus receive a drink? Did Jesus receive a drink from Jacob's well? Did the Samaritan woman provide the drink that Jesus requested? Was this statement, "give me a drink", a request that the Samaritan woman should have asked Jesus? Selah.

36 First Lady Eve and the Samaritan Woman
. . . I did eat. (Genesis 3:13b); . . Sir, give me this water. (Saint John 4:15)

Let's compare and contrast the events centered on the conversations of First Lady Eve in the Garden of Eden and the Samaritan woman at Jacob's well. The Samaritan woman at Jacob's well and First Lady Eve in the Garden of Eden were very inquisitive biblical characters. Both female characters had very intense and crucial dialogue and encounters with the Supreme Being which had everlasting effects on and implications for mankind. However, the dialogue with both biblical characters took place in two different dispensations with different persons of the Godhead in operation. First Lady Eve had a conversation with God and the adversary, the serpent, while the Samaritan woman had a conversation with Jesus during his dispensation. Let's take a look.

First Lady Eve of the Garden of Eden, the first of her kind, was made from the rib of man and made for man (Genesis 2:22). She was indeed the true First Lady who was created perfectly and sinlessly. First Lady Eve's encounter occurred in the Old Testament dispensation. This conversation occurred with God and the serpent shortly after the formation of the world. Adam and First Lady Eve talked daily and directly to God. They patrolled and delighted themselves in the Garden of Eden and did not labor for their food, shelter or clothing, as they didn't wear any clothing.

The Samaritan woman at Jacob's well was an experienced woman in the ways of life. She was different from First Lady Eve in that she was born in sin and shaped in iniquity; therefore, because of the fall of man in the dispensation of the Old Testament, she was not born perfect or sinless. However, the Samaritan woman was wonderfully and beautifully created as all of God's women are. She was beautiful and shrewd in that she attracted six men, in which five men found her worthy of marriage. Her beauty was indeed rare.

According to my interpretation of the story, the Samaritan woman's heart was not hardened by her calamities in life and disastrous marriages; however, she was very cautious as she wanted to know Jesus' credentials before she shared with him either a drink from the well and/or her life story. She was a woman of character in that she submitted to Jesus' assistance and was receptive to Jesus' gifts. She could have been very bitter toward men because of her disastrous marriages. This alone could have resulted in her rejecting Jesus and the living water. The Samaritan woman's encounter occurred in the New Testament dispensation. This conversation occurred with Jesus shortly after Jesus rested at Jacob's well from a tiresome journey.

The Samaritan woman was a woman who labored daily. The setting of this story unfolded when the Samaritan woman went to Jacob's well to draw water at an early time of the day, the sixth hour. The Samaritan woman, the weaker vessel had to carry the water pots from a great distance to Jacob's well before filling them with water. Then she had to exert her strength and energies to deliver the water container(s) back to a different destination. This in term rendered her tired from what we call today, manual labor.

The conversation with the Samaritan woman and Jesus occurred early in the heat of the day as opposed to God's conversation with Adam and First Lady Eve which occurred in the cool of the day. In this plot, both the Samaritan woman and Jesus were on a mission. Jesus had a need to go through Samaria (Saint John 4:4) and stop at Jacob's well at the sixth hour in order that the Samaritan woman may have an opportunity for spiritual fulfilment and to have her thirst quenched with the living water. The Samaritan woman had a need to go to Jacob's well at the sixth hour. Although the Samaritan woman's need was to draw water from the well to fill the pots, Jesus' need for the Samaritan woman was to draw living water from him that she shall never thirst again; but, she shall have in her a well of water springing up to everlasting life" (Saint John 4:13-14).

First Lady Eve and the Samaritan woman both had a thirst. Both biblical characters had a thirst or needs that are symbolic of the thirst women face today. The thirst both women experienced was an internal thirst that was quenched or satisfied from perhaps, an external source. First Lady Eve thirst for knowledge and received more than a quench for her thirst. The knowledge that she received as a result of eating from the forbidden tree was contrary to the knowledge that God has imparted into her. According to Genesis 3:13b, "the woman (First Lady Eve) said, the serpent beguiled me and I did eat. Eve's thirst was quenched with misinformation or mis-education as she was deceived by the serpent and ate from the forbidden tree." Why First Lady Eve didn't perceived and discerned that the serpent was a deceiver?

The Samaritan woman thirsted for spiritual fulfillment. She received more than a quench for her thirst. The living water that she received from Jesus was a restoration of virtue, spiritual fulfilment and liberation of the racial barriers that existed between the Jews and the Samaritans. "The woman (Samaritan woman) saith until him, Sir, give me this water, that I thirst not, neither come hither to draw" (Saint John 4:15). The Samaritan woman's thirst was indeed quenched so much so that she perceived and discerned that Jesus was a prophet.

Jesus' view of the Samaritan woman was quite different from our view of the Samaritan woman. It had already been established that she was a hard worker. However, at one point, if not at the conclusion of the matter, the Samaritan woman had to be a virtuous woman (Proverbs 31). If five men took her as a wife, she had some virtue about herself. The Samaritan woman respected the law of the land according to I Corinthians 7:1-2 that says "let every woman have her own husband." She remarried four times, in my opinion, attempting to remain virtuous. The justification for the four or five divorces was not discussed; neither will I speculate about it. However, the Samaritan woman engaged in an affair with the sixth man. The reason was not mention; neither will I speculate about it. Selah.

Jesus viewed the Samaritan woman as one who needed restoration and spiritual fulfilment. Jesus not only wanted to quench the woman thirst with living water, but also to refill her with the virtue that was misplaced or distorted because of the five husbands and the affair. This woman was virtuous indeed, for she realized that she had a need that only could be met by the superman which was the seventh man, Jesus. Now, where were the five husbands and the sixth man who also had need and therefore needed spiritual fulfillment? Where is the man who will point out the sins of this once virtuous woman? He who has not sinned, please cast the first stone. Selah.

Today, women face many issues in life that result in them abiding in dry, parched places. Like biblical characters First Lady Eve and the Samaritan woman, women who are married, single women who have never married, women who have been married and divorced once or more, women who have been separated and women who have lived ungodly lifestyles, have thirsts and needs that can only be filled with spiritual fulfillment and an intimate relationship with the one who is able to give the "living water." The Samaritan woman, like women today, was a woman with unfulfilled needs. The Samaritan woman chose marriage as a lifestyle for five marriages and thereby, opposed a lifestyle of fornication or as Gomer, a lifestyle of whoredom (Hosea 2:2). The Samaritan woman could have been a biblical character who married and remained divorced; she could have been a divorced character who thereafter, gave all married women nightmares or became a thorn in the flesh of women by being an adulterous woman. Nonetheless, the Samaritan woman was the biblical character that she was. The Samaritan woman's story has profound effects on and implications for womankind. Let us become vicarious learners and thereby, grasp the moral of this story. For Jesus stood and cried, saying, "In the last days, that great day of the feast, if any man thirst, let him come unto me and drink" (Saint John 7:37).

Life becomes such a daily challenge for women who were married and divorced from pastor. Former pastors' wives often question the issues that surrounded the divorce. Oftentimes, they may feel alienated from the church family in which they were First Lady. These women may be treated less than the godly women who they are; the church family may have had a tendency to judge them and the marriage from their perspective. But, as Fenwick English coined the phrase concerning "perception and reality," perception is not reality; truth is reality. Truth as it is recorded in the bible is reality and that truth becomes an absolute. Furthermore, people often view the world as "they are" not as "it is". In turn, the viewers' perception becomes their reality.

Former pastors' wives, please don't doubt yourself and your calling of a pastor's wife and/or a woman of excellence. Continue to be the virtuous woman who you are. You were wife primarily and First Lady or pastor's wife secondarily. Be encourage and lift up your head; the King of Glory shall come into your life and make it more victorious than it has ever been. The internal battles that you fought as wife and First Lady have been won.

Comfort ye, comfort ye, former pastor's wife, your warfare in the marriage is accomplished. Be comforted, O ye First Ladies, the adversary has given the pastors double trouble for accepting the call to preach and for proclaiming the gospel. You embraced and supported the pastor when you were wife and First Lady. Continue to be the godly woman of excellence who you are and continue to pray for the pastor. You know him better than anyone. And if you are a First Lady and a minister, your warfare of fighting within is accomplished. Now, go forth in the Spirit of God's might as God restores your virtue and strength. Whether the divorced occurred because of "cause, no cause or just call," I'll say to you what was said to Israel and unto me:

> (4) Fear not; for thou shall not be ashamed: neither be thou confounded; for thou shalt not be put to shame: for thou shalt forget the shame of thy youth, and shalt not remember the reproach of the widowhood any more.

> (5) For thy Maker is thine husband: the Lord of hosts is his name; and thy Redeemer the Holy One of Israel; The God of the whole earth shall be called.

> (6) For the Lord hath called thee as a woman forsaken and grieved in spirit, and a wife of youth, when thou wast refused, saith thy God (Isaiah 54:4-6).

Furthermore, God will also give unto you beauty for ashes, the oil of joy for mourning, the garment of praise for the spirit of heaviness; that you might be called trees of righteousness, the planting of the Lord, that he might be glorified (Isaiah 61:3). Hallelujah, Praise Him.

37 Jesus' Thirst and Eve's Thirst

Jesus knowing that all things were now accomplished, that the scripture might be fulfilled, saith, I thirst. Saint John 19:28 The woman said, The serpent beguiled me and I did eat. Genesis 3:13b

Let's compare and contrast the events centered around Jesus' thirst on the cross at Calvary and First Lady Eve's thirst in the Garden of Eden. In comparing and contrasting Jesus' thirst with Eve's thirst, one will find that Adam and Eve were made in the image and likeness of God (Genesis 1:26-27). They were made perfect as Jesus was. However, Jesus, the second Adam, being made flesh from the Word (Saint John 1:14), came only and after the First Adam and the First Lady Eve failed to fulfill God the Father's plan of redemption. Jesus came to fulfill the scripture (Saint John 19:28) and the ultimate purpose of God His Father (Saint John 3:16).

God placed First Man Adam in the Garden of Eden to dress and keep it (Genesis 1:15). After which, God gave First Man Adam a commandment.

> 16   "And the Lord God commanded the man, saying, of every tree of the garden thou mayest eat:
>
> But of the tree of the knowledge of good and evil, thou shalt not eat of it: for in the day that thou eatest

thereof thou shalt surely die" (Genesis 2:16-17).

However, after God blessed First Man Adam and First Lady Eve, God gave them both commandments. God said unto them:

> 28 "Be fruitful, and multiply, and replenish the earth, and subdue it: and have dominion over the fish of the sea, and over the fowl of the air, and over every living thing that moveth upon the earth.

> 29 And God said, Behold I have given you herb bearing seed, which is upon the face of all the earth, and every tree, in the which is the fruit of a tree yielding seed; to you it shall be for meat" (Genesis 1:28-29).

Let's examine the commandment God gave to First Man Adam. God specifically told Adam to freely eat from every tree in the Garden of Eden except the tree of knowledge of good and evil (Genesis 2:16-17). Now, God endowed First Man Adam and First Lady Eve with all the knowledge they needed to pastor the Garden of Eden. Adam and Eve were endowed and blessed from God with the knowledge of how to be fruitful and multiply, how to replenish and subdue the earth and how to have dominion over every living thing and creature in the Garden of Eden. The knowledge that God imparted into Adam and Eve was knowledge of good. Remember, Adam and Eve were made in God's image and likeness; therefore, they had the knowledge of "good" given to them from God who is "good."

Initially, First Man Adam and First Lady Eve were not imparted with the knowledge of evil; there wasn't a need for Adam and Eve to have the knowledge of evil nor an activation of the knowledge of evil. First Man Adam and First Lady Eve walked around in the Garden of Eden nude and thought no evil and knew no evil about their nakedness for they had no shame (Genesis 2:25). However, when God blessed (them), First Man Adam and First Lady Eve in the Garden, God gave them both the same commandment. God specifically told them to eat the fruit for meat from every tree that yield seed (Genesis 1:28-29). Therefore, First Lady Eve was given the same commandments that First Man Adam was given. Yes, God told First Lady Eve to eat the fruit for meat only from every tree that yield seed (Genesis 1:28-29). The tree of knowledge of good and evil did not produce fruit for meat that yield seed.

> 9   "And the Lord God made all kinds of trees grow out of the ground— trees that were pleasing to the eye and good for food. In the middle of the garden were the tree of life and the tree of the knowledge of good and evil" ([Genesis 2:9]; Barker, 1995).

Had the tree of knowledge of good and evil produced fruit that yield seed, its fruit would have been declared good for meat by God (Genesis 3:6); furthermore, God's commandment to Adam and Eve concerning the tree of knowledge of good and evil would have been inclusive of the trees that yield seeds.

There are questions that I ponder concerning the tree of life and the tree of knowledge of good and evil. Exactly, what did the tree of life produce? Did the tree of life produce fruit? Did the tree of life produce fruit for meat that did not yield seeds? What type of fruit did the tree of life produce? Was the tree of life symbolic in nature? Why didn't First Lady Eve choose to partake of the tree of life? Why didn't the serpent beguile Lady Eve to eat from the tree of life? Was the tree of life not pleasant to the eye? Was the tree of life not desirable to cause one to have everlasting life? Did the tree of life produce everlasting life? Why were there not a commandment concerning the tree of life? What was the purpose of the tree of life? Selah.

Now, let's take a look at the tree of knowledge of good and evil. What was so enticing about the tree of knowledge of good and evil? How did the serpent beguiled First Lady Eve to eat from the tree of knowledge of good and evil and not partake from the tree of life? Did Eve ever question or doubt have everlasting life? What was the purpose of the tree of knowledge of good and evil? Selah.

The trees in the Garden of Eden that were good for meat were in essence, good like God had made First Man Adam and First Lady Eve good. The analogy of the trees yielding seed was like unto Adam and Eve being fruitful and multiplying. The trees were good for meat in that they yield seeds or fruits, like Adam and Eve were commanded to be fruitful and multiply and to replenish the earth. The analogy of the fruits from trees yielding seeds was liken unto Jesus being the seed of God that passed through fourteen generations who became fruitful, then died and replenished the earth with His kind (Saint John 17:12-15). The analogy of the trees that produced fruits that yield seeds was like unto Christians, united to Jesus, the vine (Saint John 15:1), who are laborers in the vineyard and producers of fruit, a harvest, that remain (Saint John 15:16).

First Lady Eve desired and thirsted after knowledge. However, God had already imparted into her the "knowledge of good" that was needed in the Garden of Eden. Did Eve not know that she possessed and operated in the knowledge in which she thirsted? Did Eve not know that she had the greatest impartation of knowledge that was needed in that dispensation? Did Eve have a problem with the truth? Did First Lady Eve lack wisdom? Was she like Lucifer, wanting to have it all? Was she like Lucifer, wanting to have what

God had? Was First Lady Eve's agenda to become a little god or the God? Selah.

First Lady Eve was seduced and tempted by the serpent to eat of the tree of knowledge of good and evil (Genesis 3:1-6). Lady Eve was enticed and drawn toward the tree of good and evil with her own lust for knowledge (I James 1:14-15).

> 4 "And the serpent said unto the woman, ye shall not surely die:
>
> 5 For God doth know that in the day ye eat thereof, then your eyes shall be opened, and ye shall be as gods, knowing good and evil.
>
> 6 And when the woman saw that the tree was good for food, and that it was pleasant to the eyes, and a tree to be desired to make one wise, she took of the fruit thereof, and did eat, and gave unto her husband with her; and he did eat" (Genesis 3:4-6).

First Lady Eve thirsted after knowledge; for she desired to be wise. Eve and Adam partook willfully from the tree of knowledge of good and evil. Although they were pastors over the Garden of Eden to dress and keep it, Adam and Eve did not become as gods, in the manner that the serpent lead Lady Eve to believe. Yes, their eyes were opened and they were given the impartation of the knowledge of evil; therefore, they immediately knew evil as well as good (Genesis 3:4-5).

First Lady Eve perused over the consequences of one significant concept in her conquest for knowledge. God commandment to Adam was ". . . . For in the day that thou eatest thereof thou shalt surely die" (Genesis 2:17). However, in dialogue with First Lady Eve and the serpent, Lady Eve not only repeated this commandment that was supposedly given only to Adam, but she added to the commandment. Lady Eve stated,

> 3 "But of the fruit of the tree which is in the midst
> of the garden, God hath said, Ye shall not eat of it,
> neither shall ye touch it, lest ye die" (Genesis 3:3).

First Lady Eve added to the commandment, "Neither shall ye touch it."

First Lady Eve was given the commandment that Adam was given when he communicated that commandment to Eve. First Man Adam communicated to Lady Eve concerning this commandment. Adam shared the commandment with First Lady Eve; therefore, Eve was aware of the commandment and knew the commandment. Eve, thereby, repeated and added to the commandment.

Jesus, the second Adam, came after the First Adam and the First Lady Eve, failed to fulfill God the Father's plan of redemption. Jesus came into existence to redeem mankind from the fall of man in the Garden of Eden. Jesus thirsted to fulfill the commandment that God our Father gave him to accomplish. Jesus' thirst was definitely and infinitely quenched when he fulfilled the work which His father gave him to do" (Saint John 17:4). Jesus fulfilled the scripture (Saint John 19:28) and the ultimate purpose of God His Father (Saint John 3:16). Jesus accomplished his mission and the will of God for man which caused the Rise of Man or the right for man to have eternal life.

First Lady Eve' thirst for knowledge and the desire to fulfilled this thirst caused the Fall of Man in the Garden of Eden; this willful and disobedience act caused mankind to receive the wages of sin, the death penalty. King Jesus' thirst to fulfill the scripture caused man to rise above sin; this willful and obedience act caused man to receive the gift of God which is eternal life.

38 | Thirst - Give Me to Drink

Jesus knowing that all things were now accomplished, that the scripture might be fulfilled, saith, I thirst. Saint John 19:28 there cometh a woman of Samaria to draw water: Jesus saith unto her, Give me to drink. Saint John 4:7

Let's compare and contrast the events centered on Jesus' declaration that he thirsted and Jesus' acknowledgment that he thirsted. In both episodes in the New Testament, Jesus had just completed very significant missions; he articulated his thirst and the need for a drink after he had fulfilled his appointed missions. Again, Jesus fulfilled the needs of mankind before he met his very own personal and physical needs.

In Saint John 19:28, when Jesus declared that he thirsted as he hung nailed to the cross at Calvary, he had just completed a divine mission that had been prophesied in the Old Testament (Isaiah 52, 53) and had been fulfilled in the New Testament (Saint John 19:28). The outcome of this divine mission altered the course of history and provided mankind with a right to experience eternal life. In Saint John 4:7, when Jesus asked the Samaritan woman to "give him to drink" at Jacob's well, Jesus had just completed a divine mission that had far reaching implications, both in the arenas of morality and liberality and for racial and gender barriers that we face even today.

In both episodes, Jesus had physically exhausted himself by exerting energies and strength and by submitting his will to do the will of God his Father. In Saint John 19:28, Jesus died for the sins of the world which was the greatest gift ever given to mankind. In Saint John 4:7, Jesus offered the Samaritan woman living water which was the greatest gift that could be given to one who thirsted. In both scriptures, Jesus offered to mankind what others could not or did not do. Jesus offered everlasting life to the world by dying on the cross at Calvary (Saint John 3:16) and everlasting life to the Samaritan woman by offering her the living water at Jacob's well (Saint John 4:13-15).

In the examination of the scriptures (Saint John 19:28 and 4:7), Jesus voluntarily admitted that he had a need. Jesus communicated his needs to the very ones whom he came into the world to assist. Jesus articulated that he thirsted to the very soldiers who nailed and crucified him to the cross. In spite of the torture Jesus had experienced from the ones who nailed him to the cross, he had positive interchanged and dialogue with them. Furthermore, Jesus did not drink the vinegar and gall that the soldiers gave him to drink as he stood nailed to the cross at Calvary (In Matthew 27:34).

Jesus requested a drink from a Samaritan woman, one who didn't have an acceptable relationship with the

Jews. Despite the fact that the Samaritan woman was ostracized from the community and the fact that social and racial barriers existed between the Samaritans and the Jews, Jesus interacted and interchanged with the Samaritan woman at Jacob's well. However, it was not mentioned that he drank any liquids from the Samaritan woman at Jacob's well.

The subservience displayed by Jesus in the aforementioned events, showed forth his true awesomeness, his character and his nature. Jesus knew that the very need or element that he requested of man, was the essence of what he offered man. Jesus offering was not just contemporarily or temporarily; Jesus offered mankind an eternal gift, eternal life (Saint John 17:2).

Jesus thirsted on two occasions in the accented text. Let's ponder over questions concerning the incidents that were not answered. Was Jesus' thirst quenched? How was his thirst quenched? Who quenched Jesus' thirst? With what was his thirst quenched? When was his thirst quenched? Where was Jesus' thirst quenched? Selah.

Jesus' thirst was quenched. Jesus' thirst was quenched in that Jesus fulfilled the thirst of others. Jesus was a very compassionate and wise man. He was compassionate in that he fought a good fight for mankind and for God our

Father. Jesus was wise in that he knew his course was finished. He knew God would be glorified when he fulfilled the destiny of His Father. When Jesus was nailed to the cross at Calvary, Jesus shared his testimony concerning the fulfillment of his earthly mission.

> "Jesus knowing that all things were accomplished concerning his purpose and that the scriptures were fulfilled, saith he thirst" (Saint John 19:28).

Jesus further stated that, "I have glorified thee on the earth: I have finished the work which thou gave me to do" (Saint John 17:4).

Within these scriptures, Jesus testified that he had completed the work that His Father had appointed him to do. The works that Jesus testified concerning, consisted of and certainly not limited to: (1) God the Father, ultimately, sending his son into the world to be crucified for the sins of the world (Saint John 3:16), and; (2) Jesus teaching in the synagogues, preaching the gospel, healing sicknesses and diseases and living a holy life (Saint Matthew 4:23 and Acts 10:38). Jesus lifted up his eyes to heaven, and said,

> "Father, the hour is come" (Saint John 17:1). "And now, O Father, glorify thou me with thine own self with the glory which I had with thee before the world was (Saint John 17:5-12).

Jesus thirst was definitely and infinitely quenched when he fulfilled the work which His father gave him to do" (Saint John 17:4). Ultimately, Jesus thirsted to: (1) Complete the work the Father gave him to do (Saint John 17:4); (2) Return back to the Father; (3) Glorify God the father (Saint John 17:4), and; (4) Share the glory with his Father as one (Saint John 17:1;5).

Yes, Jesus' thirst was quenched when he fulfilled his divine purpose for existing. Jesus' thirst was quenched when he ascended back into heaven to sit on the right side of his Father. Further, Jesus' thirst was quenched when God the Father received the glory from Jesus' accomplished mission. Lastly, Jesus' thirst was definitely and infinitely quenched as He and His Father shared the Glory as one entity.

PART TEN

39 They Shall Be Filled

Blessed are they which do hunger and thirst after righteousness: for they shall be filled(Saint Matthew 5:6)

The knowledge and truth that my Tree thirsted for was the revelation knowledge, wisdom and mysteries that the Holy Spirit reveals only to His called, chosen and elected ones. In essence, My Tree searched for knowledge and truth through utility of a carnal, non-transformed mind rather than through connecting with the Holy Spirit.

In First Timothy 2:4-6, Paul speaks about the knowledge of the truth. The knowledge of the truth in this passage reference God and Jesus Christ as does the passage in Saint John 17. However, God has made the knowledge and truth or the knowledge of the truth so plain that even the simple could understand and thereby believe by faith. Paul says:

> 4 "Who will have all men to be saved, and to come unto the knowledge of truth.
>
> 5 For there is one God, and one mediator between God and men, the man Christ Jesus.
>
> 6 Who gave himself a ransom for all, to be

testified in due time."

Conclusively, Jesus states that the knowledge of the truth is to know that there is one God and one Mediator, Jesus Christ. Paul also states that the mediator, Jesus is positioned between God and man. This mediator, the intercessor, gave himself a ransom for the world. This eminent act serves as the foundation and apex of knowledge and truth or of the knowledge of the truth.

In Jesus' prayer of glorification for himself and His Father (Saint John 17), Jesus spoke expressively and prayed fervently about the acquisition of knowledge and truth. However, this knowledge and truth are grounded in knowing the one and only true God and His son, Jesus Christ. Furthermore, one must comprehend the concept of knowledge of the truth or knowing what is true concerning God and Jesus Christ.

Jesus outlined a solution as to how one may obtain this knowledge and truth. Jesus also gave a concrete definition of eternal life which encompassed the concepts of knowledge and truth. Jesus uttered:

> 3 "And this is eternal life, that they might know thee the only true God, and Jesus Christ whom thou hast sent" (Saint John 17:3).

17 "Sanctify them through thy truth: thy word is true" (Saint John 17:17).

Within the context of this scripture, Jesus specifically addressed these two main concepts: knowledge and truth. This passage is interpreted to mean that when one knows or have knowledge of whom God and Jesus are then and only, will one receive eternal life. This knowing or knowledge of God occurs only through a personal and intimate relationship with God. This passage further implies that one must spend quality time studying and meditating on the Word.

This definition of eternal life suggested that one must discern through the Holy Spirit that there is only one true God. One further must discern that the one and only true God sent His son, Jesus Christ, into the world. Essentially, if one is to have eternal life, one must believe in Saint John 3:15-16:

15 "That whosoever believeth in him should not perish, but have eternal life.

16 For God so loved the world, that he gave his only begotten Son, that whosoever believeth in him should not perish, but should have everlasting life.

As God quenched the thirst of Jesus, God also made

provision for every man's thirst to be quenched. As Jesus quenched the thirst of the Samaritan woman, Jesus also became the provision for every man thirst to be quenched. Often times, man is beguiled by satan and thereby allows satan to quench his thirst as First Lady Eve allowed. The thirst that satan quenches is unlike the thirst that Jesus quenches which lead to a well of water springing up to everlasting life" (Saint John 4:13-14); the thirst satan quenches lead to a bottomless pit that results in everlasting damnation. Other times, man is so desperate that he allows satan to quench his thirst as the Samaritan woman allowed.

The knowledge that my husband thirsted for, was in my opinion, the deep revelation and mysteries of God that the Holy Spirit reveals to only a few...His called, chosen and elected ones. In essence, My Tree searched for the knowledge of God through utility of the carnal mind, the non-transformed mind.

40 Restore My Soul

During my scheduled Bible study and meditation time, I read the Twenty-Third Psalm of David. As I read and meditated on the Word, My Shepherd, my Adonai, quietly baptized me with His oil as His presence filled the room of my home and soul. Truly my cup over-filled. I was in awesome wonder, as I basked in His presence.

My Shepherd taught me about the restoration of the soul, zoe. As 1 John 2:27 proclaimed,

> "But the anointing which ye have received of him abides in you, and ye need not that any man teach you: but as the same anointing teaches you all things, and is truth, and is no lie, and even as it has taught you, ye shall abide in him."

The anointing timely taught me the word that fulfilled a present need. For at this juncture in my life, I was in need and desired complete restoration of my brokenness.

The Lord, My Shepherd and my Adonai, filled my frail temple with His power of healing and consolation. He fulfilled the office of pastor in my life. The Greek word for Shepherd, poimen (poy-mane), means pastor (Strong, 1996). Pastor, poimen, is used metaphorically of Christian's pastors who are called to guide and feed a flock (Vine,

1996). For the shepherd or pastor of my physical life was absent. However, I was not pastorless for my spiritual Pastor and Guide filled the gap. Hallelujah!

The Lord addresses all my spiritual and social needs and desires with a familiar scripture. Simultaneously, He met all my psychological and emotional needs and scars with the power of healing. At this intense moment, all my wants were met; I did not want. I was ultimately satisfied and sanctified, too.

The Lord, my Pastor started the process of restoring my soul. The wounds and bruises to my life, my soul, for the past four years were unbearable for me, but not my God, my Adonai. God's word stated, "He will put no more on you than you can bear; and he will make a way for you to escape." Jesus was bruised and wounded for us all; but the bruisedness and the woundedness became a reality for me during the duration of this marriage.

41 Death Has No Stain

I remember one late October night in 1994. The sky was clear and the moon was full. The air was thick as the nightness, the principalities and powers that rule the air, anticipated this event. However, God altered the conclusion of this grand finale. The Lord showed up mightily and timely on the scene. As I breathe my last breathe, my soul and spirit that lined my complete physical body gently snatched and firmly pulled away from my physical body as they, in the same form, ascended. I gave up and submitted to the force that tried all my life to conquer me.

I felt so dejected and ashamed not because I gave up; I felt that God had abandoned me in this ordeal. For God has never abandoned me. I was ashamed that God did not appear on the scene, so I thought.

As I reminiscence over my life, the schemata of my life flashed before me in very vibrant hues as I could not believe that the Lord had forsaken me. For He had never forgotten or forsaken me; therefore, I am a bit spoiled. I am very persistent when it comes to God delivering my needs, wants and desires. I have expectations and complete confidence that every time I call Jesus that He will make haste to see about me. God is that type of God to me. We have that type of relationship. I agonized in physical and spiritual pain and I grieved psychologically that God did not appeared on the scene. All my life, I honored and praised God. I truly believed that I was blessed and highly favored by God. I knew that He knew me as I knew Him. I received the indwelling of the Holy Spirit at age five. I was born with asthma and live most of my infant life in a hospital, struggling to fight the enemy. I lived for God and declared that I would die for God if this incident meant God would get the glory.

Alas, the winds begun to blow slowly and quietly. Suddenly, the wind built up momentum and became stronger and stronger and mighty and mightily as it blew in all directions simultaneously; the wind made the sounds of an angry sea and the raging billows. Yet, there was no wind. The darkness dissipated and birthed a marvelous lightness. The pain immediately subsided and the tears vanished. The anger of the Lord was very vehement and violent as it stopped time and the pseudo-destiny in their tracks. The Lord took me by force from death grips. Death had no stain. My God, it was beautiful.

I saw three images of me: my physical body, my soul and my spirit. My physical body was heaviest as it laid there in the cold, very disappointed that God allowed the satanic force of hell to do such an injustice act to me, His child. My soulic image was very transparent and weightless, as it ascended up about five-to-seven feet; my soul took the complete and identical form of my physical body. However, it was a separate creation from my physical body. My spirit was very sheer and light-weighted with a radiant pureness as it too, ascended five-to seven feet from my physical form.

I felt so at peace, so still, so calm; I felt no pain no regrets. I heard no sound. The only sense that operated was my sight. Yet, it was not my sight. I saw all that one could normally hear, touch, taste and smell. I felt so at one with God. He and I were unified. All things operated in God's timing. For my timing and senses ceased instantaneously when my soul and spirit ascended. The experience was so pure, so God, so Holy, so Heaven.

Suddenly, I heard a voice say, "Your time is not at hand." Immediately, my spirit and soul reunited with my physical body as the warmth again clothed my triune self. I could feel the presence of my parents so very strongly. Their spiritual presence stayed with me for weeks before fading.

Many times over, I was reminded of a dream that I had. This very incident occurred in the same manner. Yet, in this incident, God altered the conclusion of this grand finale. This dream will be featured in a book that I will published later titled, Symbolic.

The deepness of this experience lingered for days as

it does now. My warfare is accomplished in this area; Jesus fought my battle and I was victorious. God allowed me the victory.

"I know the devil and the devil knows me!

I breathe God; for it was God who blew life back into me.

I feast on God, as I meditate on His Word day and night.

I live for God, dwelling in the house of God:

Inquiring about His secrets and mysteries that

are made known only to a few, His called, chosen, and

elected ones."

References

Barker, Kenneth, (1995). <u>The New International Study Bible</u>. Zondervan Publishing House, Grand Rapids, Michigan.

CON- Conybeare, W. J. <u>The Epistles of Paul</u>.

Dakes, Finis Jennings, (1992). <u>The Holy Bible</u>. Dake Bible Sales, Inc., Lawrenceville, Georgia.

MON- Montgomery, Helen Barrett. <u>The Centenary Translation: The New Testament in Modern English.</u>

Strong, J. (1996). <u>The New Strong Complete Dictionary of Bible Words.</u> Thomas Nelson Inc. Publisher.

Vine, W.E., Unger, M. F., and White, W. Jr. (1996). <u>Vine Complete Expository Dictionary of Old and New Testament Words.</u> Thomas Nelson Inc. Publisher.

<u>Webster's Ninth New Collegiate Dictionary</u>. (1987). Merriam-Webster Inc. Publishers.

Made in the USA
Columbia, SC
12 October 2024

43477403R00104